MORE MUFFINS

Also by Barbara Albright and Leslie Weiner

Mostly Muffins
Simply Scones
Completely Cookies
Totally Teabreads
Quick Chocolate Fixes
Wild About Brownies

MORE MUFFINS

72 Recipes for Moist, Delicious, Fresh-Baked Muffins

Barbara Albright
and
Leslie Weiner

ST. MARTIN'S GRIFFIN ❦ NEW YORK

Design by Nancy Resnick
Illustrations by Durell Godfrey

Library of Congress Cataloging-in-Publication Data

Albright, Barbara.
    More muffins / Barbara Albright and Leslie Weiner. —1st St.
Martin's Griffin ed.
        p.   cm.
    Includes index.
    ISBN 0-312-24313-8
    1. Muffins.   I. Weiner, Leslie.   II. Title.
TX770.M83A43 1999
641.8'15—dc21   99-34013
                                                                     CIP

First Edition: November 1999

10   9   8   7   6   5   4   3   2   1

To our husbands, Ted and Lowell,
who have consumed *more* muffins
than mere mortal men could handle.
To our children, Samantha Stone and Lauren,
who ate a lot of muffin crumbs.

❧ Contents ❧

✦ Metric and Imperial Conversions ✦

All of the recipes in *More Muffins* were tested using U.S. Customary measuring cups and spoons. Following are approximate conversions for weight and metric measurements. Results may vary slightly when using approximate conversions. Ingredients also vary from country to country. However, we wanted to include this list so you'll be able to make muffins wherever you may be.

✦ Oven Temperature Conversions ✦

Fahrenheit	Approximate Celsius (Centigrade)
300°F.	150°C.
325°F.	160°C.
350°F.	175°C.
375°F.	190°C.
400°F.	200°C.
425°F.	220°C.
450°F.	230°C.

❧ VOLUME CONVERSIONS ❧

U.S. Customary	Approximate Metric Conversion (ml)
⅛ teaspoon	0.5 ml
¼ teaspoon	1.0 ml
½ teaspoon	2.5 ml
1 teaspoon	5.0 ml
1 tablespoon (3 teaspoons)	15.0 ml
2 tablespoons	30.0 ml
3 tablespoons	45.0 ml
¼ cup (4 tablespoons)	60.0 ml
⅓ cup (5⅓ tablespoons)	79.0 ml
½ cup (8 tablespoons)	118.0 ml
⅔ cup (10⅔ tablespoons)	158.0 ml
¾ cup (12 tablespoons)	177.0 ml
1 cup	237.0 ml

❧ LENGTH CONVERSIONS ❧

U.S. Inches	Approximate Metric Conversion (cm)
⅜ inch	Scant 1 cm
½ inch	1.0 cm
⅝ inch	1.5 cm
1 inch	2.5 cm
2 inches	5.0 cm
3 inches	7.5 cm
4 inches	10.0 cm
5 inches	12.5 cm
6 inches	15.0 cm
7 inches	17.5 cm
8 inches	20.0 cm
9 inches	22.5 cm
10 inches	25.0 cm
11 inches	27.5 cm
12 inches	30.0 cm
13 inches	32.5 cm
14 inches	35.0 cm
15 inches	37.5 cm

❧ COMMONLY USED INGREDIENT CONVERSIONS ❧

ALL-PURPOSE FLOUR, UNSIFTED AND SPOONED INTO THE CUP

Volume	Ounces	Grams
¼ cup	1.1 oz	31 gm
⅓ cup	1.5 oz	42 gm
½ cup	2.2 oz	63 gm
1 cup	4.4 oz	125 gm

GRANULATED SUGAR

Volume	Ounces	Grams
1 teaspoon	.1 oz	4 gm
1 tablespoon	.4 oz	12 gm
¼ cup	1.8 oz	50 gm
⅓ cup	2.4 oz	67 gm
½ cup	3.5 oz	100 gm
1 cup	7.1 oz	200 gm

FIRMLY PACKED BROWN SUGAR

Volume	Ounces	Grams
1 tablespoon	.5 oz	14 gm
¼ cup	1.9 oz	55 gm
⅓ cup	2.6 oz	73 gm
½ cup	3.9 oz	110 gm
1 cup	7.8 oz	220 gm

UNSALTED BUTTER

Volume	Ounces	Grams
1 tablespoon	.5 oz	14 gm
¼ cup	2.0 oz	57 gm
⅓ cup	2.6 oz	76 gm
½ cup	4.0 oz	113 gm
1 cup	8.0 oz	227 gm

NUTS

Volume	Ounces	Grams
¼ cup	1.0 oz	28 gm
⅓ cup	1.3 oz	38 gm
½ cup	2.0 oz	57 gm
1 cup	4.0 oz	113 gm

‰ Introduction ‰

Fifteen years after the publication of our book *Mostly Muffins,* we are delighted that the passion for muffins continues and that we are writing a second book on this delicious topic. There were so many flavors yet to be done. Even though we are busy working moms now, making a batch of muffins can usually be squeezed in sometime during the day, and thanks to our always gracious editors, we took a while (years, in fact!) to finish these recipes.

Lots has changed with muffins in America. There are stores solely devoted to selling muffins—in fact, some of the stores have the same name as our first book. Now there are muffin pans available in every size and shape, so we've got chapters for mini and mega muffins, as well as the standard size. Consumers have become interested in muffins that are lower in fat, so we've included a chapter to help you out with muffins that were developed with a nod toward their healthfulness. (One change we've noticed is that milk without fat used to be called "skim milk." Now it's called "fat-free milk." One brand even had a second line clarifying the new terminology—"formerly skim milk.")

Included in this book is a chapter we've called Muf-Funs. These are recipes that have some sort of relationship to muffins, are fun, and taste great. Name aside, bear with us and be sure to give them a try. We've included a few spreads as well. We've had a great time making and eating *More Muffins* and we hope that you will soon be enjoying the delicious aroma of this all-new collection of muffins.

Happy baking!

❧ Making Perfect Muffins ❧

Within forty minutes or less, you can be enjoying freshly made muffins. Muffins are quick and easy to make and you probably have the ingredients on hand right now for several of the recipes.

The term "muffin" has come to include any small, cakelike baked good that is made in a muffin pan (and, admittedly, some of our creations are very much like cake). Most of our recipes are made according to the classic muffin method, but a few use other techniques. In the standard method, dry ingredients such as flour, sugar, baking powder and/or baking soda, and salt are mixed together in one bowl. In another bowl, liquid ingredients including milk, eggs, and melted butter are stirred together. A well is made in the center of the dry ingredients and the liquid ingredients are added and stirred just to combine.

Before preparing any recipe, read each one carefully. Then assemble the ingredients and equipment and prepare the pan. For best results, use good-quality ingredients, equipment, and utensils.

Our world is not standardized and muffin pan sizes are no exception. We tried to use the most common sizes of pans for developing our recipes. Most muffin batters can be used in other sizes of muffin cups, although you will probably have to fiddle a little bit with the baking times and the yields.

Measure all ingredients carefully. Be sure to use the appropriate measuring cups for dry and liquid ingredients. Use measuring spoons instead of flatware. Level off measuring spoons and dry measuring cups with the flat edge of a knife. Read measurements for liquid ingredients at eye level. (Refer to individual ingredients for specific instructions.)

For best results, position your oven rack so that the muffin pan is in the center of the oven. Or, if you are cooking more than one pan, evenly space the racks. Preheat the oven to the specified temperature and check the temperature with an oven thermometer. (Mercury thermometers work best.) Test for doneness as directed in each recipe. Oven temperatures vary, however, so check muffins at the minimum baking time recommended in each recipe to avoid overbaking, especially when trying recipes for the first time.

To create nicely textured, round-topped muffins, it's important that the batter not be overbeaten. Stir the mixture with a few strokes—a maximum of twenty—just until no streaks of dry ingredients remain. It's almost a folding motion. There will probably be small lumps in the batter, which will disappear when the muffins are baked. If nuts, fruits, or chocolate chips are to be added, they should be mixed in with one or two quick strokes.

Depending upon the components, the consistency of the muffin batter can vary widely. Some batters are pourable, while others are quite stiff. Spoon batter evenly among muffin cups lightly greased with butter, vegetable shortening, vegetable oil, or sprayed with nonstick vegetable cooking spray. Paper liners can also be used, if desired. The yield will increase because less batter will fit into each muffin cup. In some recipes, the edges surrounding the cups are greased as well so the muffins can be removed easily. Fill unused cups with a few tablespoons of water to ensure even baking and to protect your pan.

Follow the recipe directions for cooling the baked muffins. This usually includes a short cooling period on a wire rack before removing the muffins from the muffin pan to a wire rack to cool completely. It's important to let the muffins stay in their cups for a short period so they don't break apart when removed, but they should not be left in their cups for longer than ten minutes, as moisture may accumulate around their bases making them diffi-cult to remove. If you have any difficulty removing muffins, run a small metal spatula around edges.

Perfect muffins should be tender and light and have a uniform texture and moist crumb. They should be straight-sided and rounded on top. And, of course, they should taste great! (In our time, we've seen some spectacular-looking muffins with voluptuous tops. Unfortunately when we purchased them, these muffins often tasted like a bar of soap because they had so much leavener in them.)

Overbeating muffin batter will cause the gluten in the flour to overde-velop, which will toughen the texture of the muffins and may fill them full of tunnels. Generally, standard-size muffins are baked in a 350°F to 425°F oven for 15 to 30 minutes. If the oven heat is too low, the muffins may not peak properly, and too high an oven temperature can cause them to crack and peak unevenly.

It's difficult to resist freshly baked muffins and they are best when eaten right away. Store any cooled leftovers in an airtight container at room tem-perature. Always refrigerate muffins that contain cheese or meat, and refrig-erate all muffins during hot summer months. We've noted the muffins that freeze well.

To store muffins in the freezer for up to one month, wrap completely cooled muffins in plastic wrap and then in aluminum foil. Store in an airtight container for best results. Be sure to label and date the item before freezing so that you do not have any mystery packages in your freezer.

To reheat muffins, wrap them loosely in aluminum foil. Heat room tem-perature or refrigerated muffins at 250°F for 5 to 10 minutes; heat frozen muffins at 350°F for 15 to 20 minutes.

Ingredients

FLOUR

Unless otherwise specified, the recipes call for all-purpose flour, as this is the type of flour that most people have on hand. To measure any type of flour, lightly spoon the flour into the appropriate dry measuring cup. Try not to be heavy-handed. Level it off with the straight edge of a knife. Do not tap the cup or dip it into the flour or you will end up with more flour than is needed.

SUGAR

We've used granulated sugar, confectioners' sugar, and brown sugar in these recipes. In addition to adding sweetness, sugar is important to the texture of baked items. Measure granulated sugar by filling the appropriate dry measuring cup(s). Level it off with the straight edge of a knife. Measure confectioners' sugar in the same way that you measure flour. Light and dark brown sugar are basically interchangeable in recipes. Dark brown sugar will produce darker baked items. To measure brown sugar, press it firmly into the appropriate-size dry measuring cup(s) until it is level with the top edge. It should hold the form of the cup when turned out.

Store brown sugar in airtight containers in a cool place. One manufacturer recommends freezing brown sugar for lengthy storage, and most manufacturers include softening directions on the package should your brown sugar become dry and rocklike. One recommended method is to place the brown sugar in an airtight plastic container, cover the surface of the sugar with a piece of plastic wrap, and top with a folded moist paper towel. Seal the container for eight to twelve hours before removing the towel.

Whether you've had to soften your brown sugar or not, we've found that it is a good idea to squeeze the brown sugar between your fingertips as you add it to the mixture to eliminate sugar clumps in the finished product.

BAKING POWDER AND BAKING SODA

These two items are not interchangeable. Use whichever is called for in the recipe. Use double-acting baking powder, which is the type most readily available. (We have noticed that a few single-acting baking powders have been sneaking onto grocers' shelves.)

Double-acting baking powder enables leavening to occur both at room temperature and during baking. It contains two acid components, calcium phosphate and sodium aluminum sulfate, along with an alkali component, sodium bicarbonate (baking soda), and cornstarch. Adding liquid to baking powder causes a chemical reaction between the acid and alkali, forming carbon dioxide and water. Leavening occurs when heat causes carbon dioxide gas to be released into the dough or batter.

When acid ingredients (such as buttermilk, yogurt, sour cream, citrus, cranberries, and molasses) are used in baking, it is usually necessary to add baking soda (sodium bicarbonate—an alkali) to balance the acid-alkali ratio.

Make sure your baking powder and baking soda are fresh. They can lose their potency if stored past the expiration date or if moisture gets into the container.

UNSWEETENED COCOA POWDER

There are basically two types of unsweetened cocoa powder—alkalized and nonalkalized. The former has been treated with an alkali to make it less acidic. It is often called "Dutch-processed" or "European-styled." In our recipes we've used nonalkalized cocoa powder because we think it gives a richer, more robust chocolate flavor to baked items, and it is readily available. (Hershey's brown container of classic cocoa powder and Nestlé's are both nonalkalized.) Measure cocoa powder the same way that you measure flour.

SALT

Our recipes use very little salt and, when divided among servings, the amount of salt is minimal. Don't leave it out. We think you will find that just a little bit greatly enhances the flavor of most baked goods.

EGGS

Select large, uncracked eggs. Letting the egg reach room temperature before use makes it easier to incorporate them into the batter, but do not let them stand at room temperature for more than two hours. Because of the potential danger of salmonella in raw eggs, it is not advisable to taste any mixture containing uncooked eggs. Eggs should always be cooked to 160°F to reduce the risk of salmonella.

To bring refrigerated eggs to room temperature in a hurry, submerge them in a bowl of very warm water.

BUTTER

Use unsalted (often called sweet) butter in these recipes so that you can more accurately control the amount of salt in the recipe. The recipe will taste better, too. Salt acts as a preservative and may mask the flavor of butter that is past its prime. Unsalted butter has a shorter shelf like, so if you are keeping it for long periods of time, be sure to freeze it. You may substitute unsalted margarine. However, do not substitute vegetable oil and expect to get the same results.

Vanilla Extract

Use the real thing for better-tasting results. Pure vanilla adds a full, rich flavor and it often allows you to get by with a little less sugar.

Spices

Store spices in airtight containers away from light and heat. Older spices may lose their potency, so it is a good idea to date your containers at the time of purchase.

Fruits

Use the fruits called for in each recipe. For example, do not substitute chopped fresh fruit for dried fruit, and vice versa.

Peanut Butter

Use commercially prepared regular (not reduced-fat) peanut butter in our recipes. The health-food-store variety may change the texture of the recipe.

Nuts

It is a good idea to taste nuts before using them, as they can become rancid and spoil your recipes. Store nuts in airtight containers in the refrigerator or freezer. We like nuts and have used them in many recipes. If chopped nuts are supposed to be stirred into a batter or dough, you can usually leave them out if you do not care for nuts. Remember, however, that the volume will decrease if you omit the nuts.

⊰ MUFFINS ⊱

It will be hard for your family and friends to identify the secret ingredient—almond brickle chips—in these muffins.

2 cups all-purpose flour
½ cup firmly packed light brown sugar
2½ teaspoons baking powder
½ teaspoon salt
1 cup milk, at room temperature
⅓ cup (5⅓ tablespoons) unsalted butter, melted and cooled

1 large egg (at room temperature), lightly beaten
1 teaspoon vanilla extract
¾ cup almond brickle chips
½ cup chopped toasted almonds (see note)

1. Preheat oven to 400°F. Butter twelve 3 x 1¼-inch (3½- to 4-ounce) muffin cups.
2. In a large bowl, stir together flour, brown sugar, baking powder, and salt. In another bowl, stir together milk, butter, egg, and vanilla. Make a well in center of dry ingredients; add milk mixture and stir just to combine. Stir in chips and nuts.
3. Spoon batter into prepared muffin cups. Bake for 15 to 20 minutes, or until a toothpick inserted in center of one muffin comes out clean.
4. Remove muffin pan(s) to wire rack. Cool for 5 minutes before carefully removing muffins from cups; finish cooling on rack. Serve warm or cool completely and store in an airtight container at room temperature.
Makes 12 muffins

Note: To toast almonds, place them in a single layer in a jelly-roll pan or on a baking sheet and bake at 350°F for 5 to 7 minutes, shaking sheet a couple of times, until nuts are lightly browned.

You can substitute ¾ cup chopped chocolate-covered toffee bars for the almond brickle chips.

To clean melted almond brickle chips from muffin pan, fill muffin cups with very hot or boiling water and a small amount of dish detergent. Let stand for 10 minutes before washing muffin pan.

~ APRICOT WHITE CHOCOLATE WALNUT MUFFINS ~

Here is a flavor combination that is one of our favorites. If you like, substitute other dried fruits, chips, and nuts for those that are used in this recipe.

2 cups all-purpose flour
½ cup firmly packed light brown sugar
2 teaspoons baking powder
¼ teaspoon salt
¾ cup milk, at room temperature
½ cup (1 stick) unsalted butter, melted and cooled

1 large egg (at room temperature), lightly beaten
2 teaspoons vanilla extract
1 cup chopped dried apricots
1 cup white chocolate chips
¾ cup chopped walnuts

1. Preheat oven to 400°F. Butter twelve 3 x 1¼-inch (3½- to 4-ounce) muffin cups and edges surrounding the cups.
2. In a large bowl, stir together flour, brown sugar, baking powder, and salt. In another bowl, stir together milk, butter, egg, and vanilla until blended. Make a well in center of dry ingredients; add milk mixture and stir just to combine. Stir in apricots, chips, and nuts.
3. Spoon batter into prepared muffin cups. Bake for 15 to 20 minutes, or until a toothpick inserted in center of one muffin comes out clean.
4. Remove muffin pan(s) to wire rack. Cool for 5 minutes before carefully removing muffins from cups; finish cooling on rack. Serve warm or cool completely and store in an airtight container at room temperature.

These muffins freeze well.
Makes 12 muffins

The classic combination of chocolate, caramel, and pecans makes a decadent topping for these cakelike muffins.

MUFFINS

6 ounces bittersweet chocolate
¼ cup (½ stick) unsalted butter, at room temperature
1⅔ cups all-purpose flour
½ cup firmly packed light brown sugar
1 teaspoon baking soda

½ teaspoon salt
⅔ cup buttermilk, at room temperature
1 large egg (at room temperature), lightly beaten
1 teaspoon vanilla extract

TOPPINGS

18 unwrapped caramel candies
3 tablespoons milk
1 cup semisweet chocolate chips

½ cup sour cream, at room temperature
12 or more pecan halves, for garnish

1. Preheat oven to 375°F. Butter twelve 3 x 1¼-inch (3½- to 4-ounce) muffin cups.
2. *To prepare muffins:* In a microwave-safe bowl, heat bittersweet chocolate and butter in a microwave oven on High for 1 to 3 minutes, stirring halfway through cooking, until melted (or use a double boiler over hot, not simmering, water). Cool mixture at room temperature for 10 minutes.

3. In a large bowl, stir together flour, brown sugar, baking soda, and salt. In another bowl, stir together buttermilk, egg, and vanilla. Stir in melted chocolate mixture. Make a well in center of dry ingredients; add chocolate mixture and stir just to combine.
4. Spoon batter into prepared muffin cups. Bake for 15 to 20 minutes, or until a toothpick inserted in center of one muffin comes out clean.
5. Remove muffin pan(s) to wire rack. Cool for 10 minutes before carefully removing muffins from cups; finish cooling on rack.
6. *To prepare caramel and chocolate toppings:* In a small heavy saucepan, over low heat, melt caramels with milk, stirring until smooth. Cool mixture at room temperaure for 10 minutes. Refrigerate for 20 minutes, until slightly thickened.

   Meanwhile, in a microwave-safe bowl, heat chips in a microwave oven on High for 1 to 3 minutes, stirring halfway through cooking, until melted (or use a double boiler over hot, not simmering, water). Stir in sour cream until blended. Cool mixture at room temperature for 5 minutes.
7. With a sharp knife, cut a 1-inch diameter cone-shaped hole into each muffin top, approximately 1 inch deep. Spoon 1 rounded teaspoon of caramel topping in each hole. Top each muffin with 1 level tablespoon chocolate topping, dividing evenly among cooled muffins. Spread evenly over muffin tops. Decorate with nuts.
8. Refrigerate for 30 minutes, or until topping is set. Serve muffins or store in an airtight container in the refrigerator. Let muffins reach room temperature before serving.

Makes 12 muffins

These muffins are a hit with the kids. Because of the melting chunks of chocolate, they may stick a little. Use a butter knife to help loosen them from the cups.

1¼ cups all-purpose flour
1 cup uncooked old-fashioned rolled oats
½ cup granulated sugar
¼ cup firmly packed light brown sugar
2½ teaspoons baking powder
¼ teaspoon salt
½ cup milk, at room temperature

⅓ cup (5⅓ tablespoons) unsalted butter, melted and cooled
1 large egg (at room temperature), lightly beaten
1½ teaspoons vanilla extract
9 ounces bittersweet chocolate, cut into ½-inch pieces
1 cup coarsely broken walnuts

1. Preheat oven to 400°F. Butter twelve 2⅝ x 1⅛-inch (about 3-ounce) muffin cups and edges surrounding the cups.
2. In a large bowl, stir together flour, oats, sugars, baking powder, and salt. In another bowl, stir together milk, butter, egg, and vanilla until blended. Make a well in center of dry ingredients; add milk mixture and stir just to combine. Stir in chocolate chunks and nuts.
3. Spoon batter into prepared muffin cups. Bake for 15 to 20 minutes, or until a toothpick inserted in center of one muffin comes out clean.
4. Remove muffin pan(s) to wire rack. Cool for 5 minutes before carefully

removing muffins from cups; finish cooling on rack. Serve warm or cool completely and store in an airtight container at room temperature.
These muffins freeze well.
Makes 12 muffins

A muffin with a macaroon topping, this treat is perfect for desserts or snacks.

MACAROON TOPPING

2½ cups sweetened flaked coconut
⅔ cup sweetened condensed milk

⅛ teaspoon almond extract

MUFFINS

1 cup all-purpose flour
½ cup granulated sugar
¼ cup unsweetened nonalkalized cocoa powder
½ teaspoon baking soda
¼ teaspoon salt
½ cup buttermilk, at room temperature

¼ cup vegetable oil
1 large egg (at room temperature), lightly beaten
½ teaspoon vanilla extract
¼ cup miniature semisweet chocolate chips

1. Preheat oven to 350°F. Butter twelve 3 x 1¼-inch (3½- to 4-ounce) muffin cups and edges surrounding the cups.
2. *To prepare topping:* In a small bowl, stir together coconut, condensed milk, and almond extract; set aside.
3. *To prepare muffins:* In a large bowl, stir together flour, sugar, cocoa, baking soda, and salt. In another bowl, stir together buttermilk, oil, egg, and vanilla. Make a well in center of dry ingredients; add buttermilk mixture and stir just to combine. Stir in chips.

4. Spoon batter into prepared muffin cups. Stir coconut mixture and spoon evenly over tops of muffins. Bake for 20 to 25 minutes, or until a toothpick inserted in center of one muffin comes out clean.
5. Remove muffin pan(s) to wire rack. Cool for 5 minutes before carefully removing muffins from cups; finish cooling on rack. Serve warm or cool completely and store in an airtight container in the refrigerator. Let muffins reach room temperature before serving.

Makes 12 muffins

⚘ CHOCOLATE PEANUT BUTTER CHIP MUFFINS ⚘

These chocolaty muffins are chock-full of peanut butter chips. They would be a sweet start to any day and a great addition to a lunchbox.

1¾ cups all-purpose flour
¾ cup granulated sugar
½ cup unsweetened nonalkalized
  cocoa powder
2 teaspoons baking powder
½ teaspoon salt
1 cup milk, at room temperature

½ cup (1 stick) unsalted butter,
  melted and cooled
1 large egg (at room temperature),
  lightly beaten
1½ teaspoons vanilla extract
1 bag (10 ounces) peanut
  butter–flavored chips

1. Preheat oven to 375°F. Butter twelve 2⅝ x 1⅛-inch (about 3-ounce) muffin cups and edges surrounding cups.
2. In a large bowl, stir together flour, sugar, cocoa powder, baking powder, and salt. In another bowl, stir together milk, butter, egg, and vanilla until blended. Make a well in center of dry ingredients; add milk mixture and stir just to combine. Stir in chips.
3. Spoon batter into prepared muffin cups. Bake for 20 to 25 minutes, or until a toothpick inserted in center of one muffin comes out clean.
4. Remove muffin pan(s) to wire rack. Cool for 5 minutes before carefully removing muffins from cups; finish cooling on rack. Serve warm or cool completely and store in an airtight container at room temperature.

These muffins freeze well.

Makes 12 muffins

Sweet white chocolate is counter-balanced with tangy rosy cranberries in these rich muffins. They would be perfectly suited as part of a bread basket for a holiday brunch.

1¼ cups chopped fresh or thawed frozen cranberries
2 tablespoons plus ½ cup granulated sugar
2 cups all-purpose flour
2 teaspoons baking powder
½ teaspoon salt
¾ cup milk, at room temperature

½ cup (1 stick) unsalted butter, melted and cooled
2 large eggs (at room temperature), lightly beaten
2 teaspoons vanilla extract
2 cups white chocolate chips
½ cup coarsely broken walnuts and pecans

1. Preheat oven to 375°F. Butter twelve 3 x 1¼-inch (3½- to 4-ounce) muffin cups and edges surrounding the cups.
2. In a small bowl, stir together the cranberries and 2 tablespoons sugar. In a large bowl, stir together flour, remaining ½ cup sugar, baking powder, and salt. In another bowl, stir together milk, butter, eggs, and vanilla until blended. Make a well in center of dry ingredients; add milk mixture and stir just to combine. Stir in cranberry mixture, chips, and nuts.
3. Spoon batter into prepared muffin cups. Bake for 20 to 25 minutes, or until a toothpick inserted in center of one muffin comes out clean.
4. Remove muffin pan(s) to wire rack. Cool for 5 minutes before carefully

removing muffins from cups; finish cooling on rack. Serve warm or cool completely and store in an airtight container at cool room temperature. These muffins freeze well.

Makes 12 muffins

≈ CRUMB-TOPPED BANANA NUT MUFFINS ≈

A spiced brown sugar topping covers these moist banana nut muffins. Have a get-together for a new neighbor and serve a basket of these.

CRUMB TOPPING

½ cup all-purpose flour
¼ cup firmly packed light brown
   sugar

¼ teaspoon ground cinnamon
⅓ cup (5⅓ tablespoons) unsalted
   butter, chilled

BANANA NUT MUFFINS

2 cups all-purpose flour
1½ teaspoons baking powder
½ teaspoon baking soda
½ teaspoon salt
1 cup mashed ripe bananas
   (about 2 large bananas)
⅓ cup milk, at room temperature

2 teaspoons vanilla extract
½ cup (1 stick) unsalted butter,
   softened
1 cup granulated sugar
2 large eggs (at room
   temperature)
1 cup chopped walnuts (optional)

1. Preheat oven to 350°F. Butter twelve 3 x 1¼-inch (3½- to 4-ounce) muffin cups and edges surrounding the cups.
2. *To prepare crumb topping:* In a small bowl, stir together flour, brown sugar, and cinnamon. Cut butter into ½-inch cubes and distribute them over flour mixture. Using your fingertips, quickly rub butter into mixture until it resembles coarse crumbs. Set aside.

3. *To prepare banana nut muffins:* In a large bowl, stir together flour, baking powder, baking soda, and salt. In another bowl, stir together bananas, milk, and vanilla. In another bowl, using an electric mixer, cream butter and sugar until light and fluffy. One at a time, beat in eggs. In two additions each, beat in banana mixture and flour mixture just until combined. Stir in nuts, if desired.

4. Spoon batter into prepared muffin cups. Sprinkle crumb topping evenly over tops of muffins. Bake for 25 to 30 minutes, or until a toothpick inserted in center of one muffin comes out clean.

5. Remove muffin pan(s) to wire rack. Cool for 5 minutes before carefully removing muffins from cups; finish cooling on rack. Serve warm or cool completely and store in an airtight container at room temperature.

Makes 12 muffins

～ DRIED CRANBERRY ORANGE MUFFINS ～

Dried cranberries add an unusual touch to this classic flavor combination.

2 cups all-purpose flour
⅔ cup firmly packed light brown
    sugar
1 teaspoon baking powder
1 teaspoon baking soda
½ teaspoon salt
1 cup buttermilk, at room
    temperature
⅓ cup vegetable oil

1 large egg (at room temperature),
    lightly beaten
1 teaspoon vanilla extract
1 teaspoon grated orange peel
¾ cup dried cranberries
½ cup chopped walnuts or
    pecans, toasted, if desired (see
    note)

1. Preheat oven to 400°F. Butter twelve 3 x 1¼-inch (3½- to 4-ounce) muffin cups and edges surrounding the cups.
2. In a large bowl, stir together flour, brown sugar, baking powder, baking soda, and salt. In another bowl, stir together buttermilk, oil, egg, vanilla, and orange peel. Make a well in center of dry ingredients; add milk mixture and stir just to combine. Stir in cranberries and nuts.
3. Spoon batter into prepared muffin cups. Bake for 15 to 20 minutes, or until a toothpick inserted in center of one muffin comes out clean.
4. Remove muffin pan(s) to wire rack. Cool for 5 minutes before carefully removing muffins from cups; finish cooling on rack. Serve warm or cool completely and store in an airtight container at room temperature.

Makes 12 muffins

Note: To toast walnuts or pecans, place them in a single layer in a jelly-roll pan or on a baking sheet and bake at 350°F for 5 to 7 minutes, shaking sheet a couple of times, until nuts are lightly browned.

Dried cranberries are often available in gourmet food stores and some supermarkets. Chopped pitted dates may be substituted for the dried cranberries.

⁂ Lemon Buttermilk Muffins with Crumb Topping ⁂

A generous crumb topping spills over the edges of these muffins, just begging to be broken off and snacked on. These muffins are a natural with tea.

Crumb Topping

1 cup all-purpose flour
½ cup firmly packed light brown sugar

½ cup (1 stick) unsalted butter, chilled

Lemon Buttermilk Muffins

2 cups all-purpose flour
1 cup granulated sugar
1 teaspoon baking powder
1 teaspoon baking soda
¼ teaspoon salt
1 cup buttermilk, at room temperature

½ cup (1 stick) unsalted butter, melted and cooled
1 large egg (at room temperature), lightly beaten
2 teaspoons grated lemon peel
1½ teaspoons vanilla extract

1. Preheat oven to 400°F. Butter twelve 3 x 1¼-inch (3½- to 4-ounce) muffin cups and edges surrounding the cups.
2. *To prepare crumb topping:* In a small bowl, stir together flour and brown sugar. Cut butter into ½-inch cubes and distribute them over flour mixture.

27

Using your fingertips, quickly rub butter into mixture until it resembles coarse crumbs. Set aside.

3. *To prepare lemon buttermilk muffins:* In a large bowl, stir together flour, sugar, baking powder, baking soda, and salt. In another bowl, stir together buttermilk, butter, egg, lemon peel, and vanilla. Make a well in center of dry ingredients; add buttermilk mixture and stir just to combine.

4. Spoon batter into prepared muffin cups. Sprinkle crumb topping evenly over tops of muffins. Bake for 15 to 20 minutes, or until a toothpick inserted in center of one muffin comes out clean.

5. Remove muffin pan(s) to wire rack. Cool for 5 minutes before carefully removing muffins from cups; finish cooling on rack. Serve warm or cool completely and store in an airtight container at room temperature.

Makes 12 muffins

ᘓ More-Crumb-Than-Muffin Muffins with Optional Chocolate Drizzle ᘓ

If you like crumb toppings that are thick, here's the one for you. For extra decadence, drizzle swirls of chocolate over the tops of the muffins.

CRUMB TOPPING

1½ cups all-purpose flour
¾ cup firmly packed light brown sugar

½ teaspoon ground cinnamon
½ cup (1 stick) unsalted butter, melted

MUFFINS

1¼ cups all-purpose flour
½ cup granulated sugar
1½ teaspoons baking powder
¼ teaspoon salt
½ cup milk, at room temperature

⅓ cup (5⅓ tablespoons) unsalted butter, melted and cooled
1 large egg (at room temperature), lightly beaten
1½ teaspoons vanilla extract

CHOCOLATE DRIZZLE (OPTIONAL)

3 ounces bittersweet chocolate, coarsely broken

1. Preheat oven to 350°F. Butter twelve 3 x 1¼-inch (3½- to 4-ounce) muffin cups and edges surrounding the cups.

2. *To prepare crumb topping:* In a small bowl, stir together flour, brown sugar, and cinnamon. Stir in butter until combined.

3. *To prepare muffins:* In a large bowl, stir together flour, sugar, baking powder, and salt. In another bowl, stir together milk, butter, egg, and vanilla until blended. Make a well in center of dry ingredients; add milk mixture and stir just to combine.

4. Spoon batter into prepared muffin cups. Sprinkle crumb topping evenly over tops of muffins. Bake for 25 to 30 minutes, or until a toothpick inserted in center of one muffin comes out clean.

5. *To prepare chocolate drizzle, if using:* In a microwave-safe bowl, heat chocolate in a microwave oven on High for 1 to 2 minutes, stirring halfway through cooking until chocolate is melted (or use a double boiler over hot, not simmering, water). Drizzle chocolate over tops of baked muffins.

6. Remove muffin pan(s) to wire rack. Cool for 5 minutes before carefully removing muffins from cups; finish cooling on rack. Serve warm or cool completely and store in an airtight container at room temperature.

Makes 12 muffins

Reminiscent of old-fashioned oatmeal raisin cookies, these muffins go well with yogurt.

1 cup all-purpose flour	**½ cup milk, at room temperature**
1 cup uncooked old-fashioned rolled oats	**⅓ cup (5⅓ tablespoons) unsalted butter, melted and cooled**
½ cup firmly packed light brown sugar	**1 large egg (at room temperature), lightly beaten**
2½ teaspoons baking powder	**1½ teaspoons vanilla extract**
¼ teaspoon salt	**¾ cup raisins**

1. Preheat oven to 400°F. Butter eight 2⅝ x 1⅛-inch (about 3-ounce) muffin cups.
2. In a large bowl, stir together flour, oats, brown sugar, baking powder, and salt. In another bowl, stir together milk, butter, egg, and vanilla until blended. Make a well in center of dry ingredients; add milk mixture and stir just to combine. Stir in raisins.
3. Spoon batter into prepared muffin cups. Bake for 15 to 20 minutes, or until a toothpick inserted in center of one muffin comes out clean.
4. Remove muffin pan(s) to wire rack. Cool for 5 minutes before carefully removing muffins from cups; finish cooling on rack. Serve warm or cool completely and store in an airtight container at room temperature.

These muffins freeze well.

Makes 8 muffins

✎ PANETTONE MUFFINS ✎

Based on the Italian holiday sweet bread, this version in the form of muffins is fast and just as delicious.

2 cups all-purpose flour
⅓ cup granulated sugar
2½ teaspoons baking powder
½ teaspoon salt
¾ cup milk, at room temperature
⅓ cup (5⅓ tablespoons) unsalted butter, melted and cooled
⅓ cup sweet Marsala wine (see note)

1 large egg (at room temperature), lightly beaten
1 teaspoon vanilla extract
½ cup raisins
½ cup chopped candied fruit, such as citron (see note)
24 whole blanched almonds

1. Preheat oven to 400°F. Butter twelve 3 x 1¼-inch (3½- to 4-ounce) muffin cups.
2. In a large bowl, stir together flour, sugar, baking powder, and salt. In another bowl, stir together milk, butter, wine, egg, and vanilla. Make a well in center of dry ingredients; add milk mixture and stir just to combine. Stir in raisins and candied fruit.
3. Spoon batter into prepared muffin cups. Top each muffin with two nuts. Bake for 15 to 20 minutes, or until a toothpick inserted in center of one muffin comes out clean.
4. Remove muffin pan(s) to wire rack. Cool for 5 minutes before carefully removing muffins from cups; finish cooling on rack. Serve warm or cool

completely and store in an airtight container at room temperature. These muffins freeze well.
Makes 12 muffins

Note: Marsala is sweet Sicilian wine. Sweet sherry can be substituted.

Candied fruit, sometimes referred to as fruit and peel mix, is readily available during the holidays in November and December. If you prefer, chopped dried fruits (such as cherries, apricots, and cranberries) can be substituted for the candied fruit.

❧ PLUM YOGURT MUFFINS ❧

Bits of fresh plum add moistness to these lemon-flavored muffins. They get their refreshing citrus flavor from lemon yogurt and grated lemon peel.

2 cups all-purpose flour
¾ cup granulated sugar
1 teaspoon baking powder
½ teaspoon baking soda
¼ teaspoon salt
1 container (8 ounces) low-fat lemon yogurt, at room temperature

½ cup (1 stick) unsalted butter, melted and cooled
2 large eggs (at room temperature), lightly beaten
1½ teaspoons vanilla extract
¼ teaspoon grated lemon peel
1 cup chopped fresh plums
¾ cup slivered almonds (optional)

1. Preheat oven to 375°F. Butter twelve 3 x 1¼-inch (3½- to 4-ounce) muffin cups.
2. In a large bowl, stir together flour, sugar, baking powder, baking soda, and salt. In another bowl, stir together yogurt, butter, eggs, vanilla, and lemon peel until blended. Make a well in center of dry ingredients; add yogurt mixture and stir just to combine. Stir in plums and nuts, if desired.
3. Spoon batter into prepared muffin cups. Bake for 20 to 25 minutes, or until a toothpick inserted in center of one muffin comes out clean.
4. Remove muffin pan(s) to wire rack. Cool for 5 minutes before carefully removing muffins from cups; finish cooling on rack. Serve warm or cool completely and store in an airtight container at cool room temperature.

Makes 12 muffins

❧ RED PEPPER CHEDDAR CORN MUFFINS ❧

Try these muffins with a soup and/or salad and you've prepared a simple yet sophisticated meal.

1 cup all-purpose flour
1 cup yellow cornmeal
2 teaspoons granulated sugar
2 teaspoons baking powder
¼ teaspoon salt
1 cup shredded sharp Cheddar
   cheese
¼ cup grated Parmesan cheese

1 cup milk, at room temperature
2 large eggs (at room
   temperature), lightly beaten
¼ cup vegetable oil
⅛ teaspoon hot pepper sauce
½ cup chopped red bell pepper
¼ cup chopped scallions,
   including tender green tops

1. Preheat oven to 400°F. Butter twelve 2⅝ x 1⅛-inch (about 3-ounce) muffin cups.
2. In a large bowl, stir together flour, cornmeal, sugar, baking powder, and salt. Stir in cheeses to combine. In another bowl, stir together milk, eggs, oil, and pepper sauce until blended. Make a well in center of dry ingredients; add milk mixture and stir just to combine. Stir in bell pepper and scallions.
3. Spoon batter into prepared muffin cups. Bake for 15 to 20 minutes, or until a toothpick inserted in center of one muffin comes out clean.
4. Remove muffin pan(s) to wire rack. Cool for 5 minutes before removing muffins from cups; finish cooling on rack. Serve warm or cool completely and store in an airtight container at cool room temperature. These muffins are best served warm.

Makes 12 muffins

This is a muffin version of the favorite Viennese dessert—dense chocolate cake with apricot preserves and a chocolate glaze.

MUFFINS

7 ounces bittersweet chocolate
⅓ cup (5⅓ tablespoons) butter, at room temperature
1⅔ cups all-purpose flour
½ cup granulated sugar
1 teaspoon baking soda
½ teaspoon salt

⅔ cup buttermilk, at room temperature
1 large egg (at room temperature), lightly beaten
1½ teaspoons vanilla extract
Approximately ⅓ cup apricot preserves

CHOCOLATE GLAZE

3½ ounces bittersweet chocolate
3 tablespoons unsalted butter, at room temperature

1 tablespoon light corn syrup
Approximately ¼ cup apricot preserves

1. Preheat oven to 375°F. Butter twelve 3 x 1¼-inch (3½- to 4-ounce) muffin cups and edges surrounding the cups.
2. *To prepare muffins:* In a microwave-safe bowl, heat chocolate and butter in a microwave oven on High for 1 to 3 minutes, stirring halfway through cooking, until melted (or use a double boiler over hot, not simmering, water). Cool mixture at room temperature for 10 minutes.
3. In a large bowl, stir together flour, sugar, baking soda, and salt. In another

bowl, stir together buttermilk, egg, and vanilla. Stir in melted chocolate mixture. Make a well in center of dry ingredients; add chocolate mixture and stir just to combine.

4. Spoon 1 heaping tablespoonful (approximately 2 level tablespoons) of batter into prepared muffin cups. Spoon 1 teaspoon preserves in center of each portion of batter; do not let preserves touch sides of cups. Spoon remaining batter into cups over preserves. Bake for 15 to 20 minutes, or until a toothpick inserted in center of one muffin comes out clean.

5. Remove muffin pan(s) to wire rack. Cool for 10 minutes before carefully removing muffins from cups; finish cooling on rack.

6. *To prepare glaze:* In a microwave-safe bowl, heat chocolate and butter in a microwave oven on High for 1 to 2 minutes, stirring halfway through cooking, until melted (or use a double boiler over hot, not simmering, water). Stir in corn syrup. Cool mixture at room temperature for 5 minutes.

7. Spread scant 1 teaspoon apricot preserves over the top of each muffin. Top each muffin with 1 heaping teaspoon chocolate glaze, dividing evenly among muffin cups. Spread to cover tops of muffins. Refrigerate for 20 minutes, or until glaze is set. Serve muffins or store in an airtight container in the refrigerator. Let muffins reach room temperature before serving.

Makes 12 muffins

Make these muffins in the summer when blueberries are at their peak.

2 cups all-purpose flour
¾ cup plus 1 tablespoon
  granulated sugar
1 teaspoon baking powder
1 teaspoon baking soda
½ teaspoon salt
1 cup reduced-fat or regular sour
  cream, at room temperature

¼ cup (½ stick) unsalted butter,
  melted and cooled
1 large egg (at room temperature),
  lightly beaten
1½ teaspoons vanilla extract
2 cups blueberries

1. Preheat oven to 400°F. Butter twelve 3 x 1¼-inch (3½- to 4-ounce) muffin cups.
2. In a large bowl, stir together flour, ¾ cup sugar, baking powder, baking soda, and salt. In another bowl, stir together sour cream, butter, egg, and vanilla until blended. Make a well in center of dry ingredients; add sour cream mixture and stir just to combine. Stir in blueberries.
3. Spoon batter into prepared muffin cups and sprinkle tops with remaining 1 tablespoon sugar. Bake for 15 to 20 minutes, or until a toothpick inserted in center of one muffin comes out clean.
4. Remove muffin pan(s) to wire rack. Cool for 5 minutes before carefully removing muffins from cups; finish cooling on rack. Serve warm or cool completely and store in an airtight container at cool room temperature.

Makes 12 muffins

Praline and peaches combine to create muffins with a Southern accent.

PRALINE

⅓ **cup granulated sugar**
3 **tablespoons water**

⅔ **cup pecans**

MUFFINS

2 **cups all-purpose flour**
⅔ **cup firmly packed light brown**
   sugar
1 **teaspoon baking powder**
1 **teaspoon baking soda**
½ **teaspoon salt**
¾ **cup buttermilk, at room**
   temperature

⅓ **cup vegetable oil**
1 **large egg (at room temperature),**
   lightly beaten
1 **teaspoon vanilla extract**
¾ **cup chopped, drained, canned**
   peaches or fresh peaches

1. *To prepare praline:* Lightly oil a 10-inch-diameter circle on a baking sheet. In a small heavy saucepan, stir together granulated sugar and water. Cook over medium heat, stirring constantly, until sugar dissolves. Increase heat to high and bring mixture to a boil. Cook without stirring for 3½ minutes, or until mixture caramelizes. Immediately add nuts and stir to coat nuts with syrup. Immediately scrape mixture onto oiled part of prepared baking sheet. Cool for 20 minutes, or until hardened. Transfer mixture to a cutting board and chop praline.

2. *To prepare muffins:* Preheat oven to 400°F. Lightly butter twelve 3 x 1¼-inch (3½- to 4-ounce) muffin cups and edges surrounding the cups.
3. In a large bowl, stir together flour, brown sugar, baking powder, baking soda, and salt. In another bowl, stir together buttermilk, oil, egg, and vanilla. Make a well in center of dry ingredients; add milk mixture and stir just to combine. Stir in chopped praline and peaches.
4. Spoon batter into prepared muffin cups. Bake for 15 to 20 minutes, or until a toothpick inserted in center of one muffin comes out clean.
5. Remove muffin pan(s) to wire rack. Cool for 5 minutes before carefully removing muffins from cups; finish cooling on rack. Serve warm or cool completely and store in an airtight container in the refrigerator. Let muffins reach room temperature before serving.

Makes 12 muffins

For Pecan Muffins: Omit peaches and increase buttermilk to 1 cup. Proceed as directed above.

These muffins, studded with sun-dried tomatoes and Cheddar cheese, are a terrific accompaniment to dinner.

2 cups all-purpose flour
2½ teaspoons baking powder
½ teaspoon salt
1 cup milk, at room temperature
½ cup mashed potatoes
¼ cup (½ stick) unsalted butter, melted and cooled

1 large egg (at room temperature), lightly beaten
½ teaspoon hot pepper sauce
¾ cup (about 3 ounces) shredded sharp Cheddar cheese
¼ cup chopped sun-dried tomatoes packed in oil, drained
2 tablespoons chopped scallions

1. Preheat oven to 400°F. Butter twelve 3 x 1¼-inch (3½- to 4-ounce) muffin cups.
2. In a large bowl, stir together flour, baking powder, and salt. In another bowl, stir together milk, mashed potatoes, butter, egg, and pepper sauce. Make a well in center of dry ingredients; add milk mixture and stir just to combine. Stir in cheese, tomatoes, and scallion.
3. Spoon batter into prepared muffin cups. Bake for 15 to 20 minutes, or until a toothpick inserted in center of one muffin comes out clean.
4. Remove muffin pan(s) to wire rack. Cool for 5 minutes before carefully removing muffins from cups; finish cooling on rack. Serve warm or cool completely and store in an airtight container in the refrigerator. Let muffins reach room temperature or warm slightly before serving.

Makes 12 muffins

Chocolate and orange are blended to create a tempting flavor combination in these two-tone muffins.

2 ounces bittersweet chocolate
2 cups all-purpose flour
½ cup granulated sugar
2½ teaspoons baking powder
½ teaspoon salt
1 cup milk, at room temperature
⅓ cup (5⅓ tablespoons) unsalted
  butter, melted and cooled

1 large egg (at room temperature),
  lightly beaten
1¼ teaspoons grated orange peel
1 teaspoon vanilla extract
½ cup miniature semisweet
  chocolate chips

1. Preheat oven to 400°F. Butter twelve 3 x 1¼-inch (3½- to 4-ounce) muffin cups.
2. In a microwave-safe bowl, heat chocolate in a microwave oven on High for 1 to 2 minutes, stirring halfway through cooking, until melted (or use a double boiler, over hot, not simmering, water). Cool mixture at room temperature for 10 minutes.
3. In a large bowl, stir together flour, sugar, baking powder, and salt. In another bowl, stir together milk, butter, egg, orange peel, and vanilla. Make a well in center of dry ingredients; add milk mixture and stir just to combine.
4. Spoon about half of the batter into another bowl. Stir in melted chocolate until blended. Stir in ¼ cup of the chips. Spoon into prepared muffin cups.

5. Stir remaining ¼ cup chips into the remaining batter and spoon into muffin cups. Swirl batter with a knife, if desired. Bake for 15 to 20 minutes, or until a toothpick inserted in center of one muffin comes out clean.
6. Remove muffin pan(s) to wire rack. Cool for 5 minutes before carefully removing muffins from cups; finish cooling on rack. Serve warm or cool completely and store in an airtight container at room temperature.

Makes 12 muffins

For Two-Tone Chocolate Chip Muffins: Omit grated orange peel.

≈ ZUCCHINI MUFFINS ≈

This batter is stiffer than most; when we tested it we were afraid it wouldn't turn out. But these crunchy topped sweet muffins will not disappoint.

2 cups all-purpose flour
1 cup granulated sugar
1 tablespoon baking powder
½ teaspoon salt
1 teaspoon ground cinnamon
⅛ teaspoon ground nutmeg
⅛ teaspoon ground cloves

⅛ teaspoon ground ginger
½ cup vegetable oil
2 large eggs (at room
    temperature), lightly beaten
1 teaspoon vanilla extract
1½ cups shredded zucchini
¾ cup chopped walnuts (optional)

1. Preheat oven to 400°F. Butter twelve 2⅝ x 1⅛-inch (about 3-ounce) muffin cups.
2. In a large bowl, stir together flour, sugar, baking powder, salt, cinnamon, nutmeg, cloves, and ginger. In another bowl, stir together oil, eggs, and vanilla until blended. Make a well in center of dry ingredients; add oil mixture and stir just to combine. Stir in zucchini and nuts, if desired.
3. Spoon batter into prepared muffin cups. Bake for 20 to 25 minutes, or until a toothpick inserted in center of one muffin comes out clean.
4. Remove muffin pan(s) to wire rack. Cool for 5 minutes before carefully removing muffins from cups; finish cooling on rack. Serve warm or cool completely and store in an airtight container at cool room temperature.
    These muffins freeze well.

Makes 12 muffins

✒ Mini Muffins ✒

❧ Berry Cherry Mini Muffins ❧

Chock-full of dried blueberries and cherries, these little muffins are great to have on hand in the freezer for a lunchbox filler. Substitute an equal amount of other dried fruits and nuts for the berries and cherries for variety. Cherries and almonds would be lovely.

2 cups all-purpose flour
⅓ cup firmly packed light brown sugar
⅓ cup granulated sugar
2 teaspoons baking powder
½ teaspoon salt
⅔ cup milk, at room temperature
½ cup (1 stick) unsalted butter, melted and cooled

2 large eggs (at room temperature), lightly beaten
2 teaspoons vanilla extract
½ cup chopped dried blueberries
½ cup chopped dried cherries

1. Preheat oven to 400°F. Butter thirty-six 1¾ x ¾-inch (about 1-ounce) muffin cups.
2. In a large bowl, stir together flour, sugars, baking powder, and salt. In another bowl, stir together milk, butter, eggs, and vanilla until blended. Make a well in center of dry ingredients; add milk mixture and stir just to combine. Stir in blueberries and cherries. Spoon batter into prepared muffin cups. Bake for 15 to 20 minutes, or until a toothpick inserted in center of one muffin comes out clean.

3. Remove muffin pans to wire rack. Cool for 5 minutes before removing muffins from cups; finish cooling on rack. Serve warm or cool completely and store in an airtight container at room temperature.

These muffins freeze well.

Makes 36 mini muffins

These rich chocolate muffins with a creamy topping are sure to be a favorite with kids.

CHEESE TOPPING

1 package (3 ounces) cream
   cheese, at room temperature

1 tablespoon granulated sugar
½ teaspoon vanilla extract

MUFFINS

3½ ounces bittersweet chocolate
2 tablespoons unsalted butter
⅔ cup all-purpose flour
3 tablespoons granulated sugar
¼ teaspoon baking soda
⅛ teaspoon salt

¼ cup buttermilk, at room
   temperature
1 large egg (at room temperature),
   lightly beaten
½ teaspoon vanilla extract

1. Preheat oven to 375°F. Butter twenty-four 1¾ x ¾-inch (about 1-ounce) muffin cups.
2. *To prepare topping:* In a small bowl, stir together cream cheese, sugar, and vanilla until blended. Set aside.
3. *To prepare muffins:* In a microwave-safe bowl, heat chocolate and butter in a microwave oven on High for 1 to 2 minutes, stirring halfway through cooking, until melted (or use a double boiler over hot, not simmering, water). Cool mixture at room temperature for 10 minutes.

4. In a large bowl, stir together flour, sugar, baking soda, and salt. In another bowl, stir together buttermilk, egg, vanilla, and cooled chocolate. Make a well in center of dry ingredients; add milk mixture and stir just to combine.
5. Spoon batter into prepared muffin cups. Top each muffin with one rounded ½ teaspoonful cream cheese topping, dividing evenly among muffin cups. Bake for 10 minutes, or until a toothpick inserted in center of one muffin comes out clean.
6. Remove muffin pan(s) to wire rack. Cool for 2 minutes before carefully removing muffins from cups; finish cooling on rack. Serve warm or cool completely and store in an airtight container in the refrigerator. Let muffins reach room temperature before serving.

Makes 24 mini muffins

These mini muffins are reminiscent of babka, a rich coffee cake. They are perfect served with mugs of hot coffee or tea.

CRUMB TOPPING

3 tablespoons all-purpose flour
1 tablespoon firmly packed light
   brown sugar

⅛ teaspoon ground cinnamon
Generous dash salt
1 tablespoon butter, chilled

MUFFINS

1½ ounces bittersweet chocolate
1 cup all-purpose flour
⅓ cup granulated sugar
1 teaspoon baking powder
¼ teaspoon salt

½ cup milk
2½ tablespoons unsalted butter,
   melted and cooled
1 large egg, at room temperature
1 teaspoon vanilla extract

1. Preheat oven to 375°F. Butter eighteen 1¾ x ¾-inch (about 1-ounce) muffin cups and edges surrounding the cups.
2. *To prepare crumb topping:* In a small bowl, stir together flour, brown sugar, cinnamon, and salt. Cut butter into small cubes and distribute them over the flour mixture. With a pastry blender or two knives used scissors fashion, cut in butter until mixture resembles coarse crumbs. Set aside.
3. *To prepare muffins:* In a microwave-safe bowl, heat chocolate in a microwave oven on High for 1 to 2 minutes, stirring halfway through

cooking, until melted (or use a double boiler over hot, not simmering, water). Cool at room temperature for 10 minutes.

4. In a large bowl, stir together flour, granulated sugar, baking powder, and salt. In another bowl, stir together milk, butter, egg, and vanilla. Make a well in center of dry ingredients; add milk mixture and stir just to combine. Remove ½ cup batter to a small bowl; stir in melted chocolate until blended.

5. Spoon chocolate batter into prepared muffin cups. Spoon remaining batter into muffin cups. Swirl batter with a knife, if desired. Sprinkle crumb topping evenly over tops of muffins. Bake for 15 to 20 minutes, or until a toothpick inserted in center of one muffin comes out clean.

6. Remove muffin pan(s) to wire rack. Cool for 3 minutes before carefully removing muffins from cups; finish cooling on rack. Serve warm or cool completely and store in an airtight container at room temperature.

Makes 18 mini muffins

Delicious warm served with butter and/or honey, these muffins are also perfect when split and filled with a little honey mustard and thinly sliced smoked turkey or ham.

1 cup all-purpose flour
1 cup yellow cornmeal
⅓ cup granulated sugar
1 tablespoon baking powder
½ teaspoon salt
1 cup milk, at room temperature

½ cup (1 stick) unsalted butter,
    melted and cooled
2 large eggs (at room
    temperature), lightly beaten
1½ teaspoons vanilla extract

1. Preheat oven to 400°F. Butter thirty 1¾ x ¾-inch (about 1-ounce) muffin cups.
2. In a large bowl, stir together flour, cornmeal, sugar, baking powder, and salt. In another bowl, stir together milk, butter, eggs, and vanilla until blended. Make a well in center of dry ingredients; add milk mixture and stir just to combine.
3. Spoon batter into prepared muffin cups. Bake for 15 to 20 minutes, or until a toothpick inserted in center of one muffin comes out clean.
4. Remove muffin pans to wire rack. Cool for 5 minutes before removing muffins from cups; finish cooling on rack. Serve warm or cool completely and store in an airtight container at room temperature.

Makes 30 muffins

❧ DAISIES' CHOICE MINI M&M'S MINI MUFFINS ❧

These diminuitive muffins were developed, assembled, and baked for the discriminating Daisies of Wilton, Connecticut Girl Scout Troop 700. They received rave reviews and the recipe was deemed a "keeper." Fortunately there were enough muffins for seconds! Try them with other stir-ins such as mini chocolate chips and toffee bits. If desired, reserve ⅓ cup of the M&M's and sprinkle them evenly over the tops of the filled muffins before baking. (P.S. This was one of the first recipes we developed. The girls have now advanced to become Brownies!)

2 cups all-purpose flour
⅓ cup firmly packed light brown
  sugar
⅓ cup granulated sugar
2 teaspoons baking powder
½ teaspoon salt
⅔ cup milk, at room temperature

½ cup (1 stick) unsalted butter,
  melted and cooled
2 large eggs (at room
  temperature), lightly beaten
2 teaspoons vanilla extract
1 package (12 ounces) miniature
  M&M's

1. Preheat oven to 400°F. Butter thirty-six 1¾ x ¾-inch (about 1-ounce) muffin cups.
2. In a large bowl, stir together flour, sugars, baking powder, and salt. In another bowl, stir together milk, butter, eggs, and vanilla until blended. Make a well in center of dry ingredients; add milk mixture and stir just to combine. Stir in miniature M&M's.

3. Spoon batter into prepared muffin cups. Bake for 15 to 20 minutes, or until a toothpick inserted in center of one muffin comes out clean.
4. Remove muffin pans to wire rack. Cool for 5 minutes before carefully removing muffins from cups; finish cooling on rack. Serve warm or cool completely and store in an airtight container at room temperature.

These muffins freeze well.

Makes 36 mini muffins

The rich flavor of coffee with a hint of cinnamon makes these muffins special.

1 cup all-purpose flour
¼ cup firmly packed dark brown sugar
1¼ teaspoons baking powder
2 teaspoons instant espresso powder
¼ teaspoon ground cinnamon
⅛ teaspoon salt
½ cup milk, at room temperature
2 tablespoons vegetable oil

1 large egg (at room temperature), lightly beaten
½ teaspoon vanilla extract
¼ cup miniature semisweet chocolate chips
¼ cup chopped toasted blanched hazelnuts (see note)
Toasted blanched hazelnuts for garnish (optional)

1. Preheat oven to 400°F. Butter twenty-one 1¾ x ¾-inch (about 1-ounce) muffin cups.
2. In a large bowl, stir together flour, sugar, baking powder, espresso powder, cinnamon, and salt. In another bowl, stir together milk, oil, egg, and vanilla. Make a well in center of dry ingredients; add milk mixture and stir just to combine. Stir in chips and chopped nuts.
3. Spoon batter into prepared muffin cups. Garnish each muffin with a whole hazelnut, if desired. Bake for 10 minutes, or until a toothpick inserted in center of one muffin comes out clean.

4. Remove muffin pan(s) to wire rack. Cool for 2 minutes before carefully removing muffins from cups; finish cooling on rack. Serve warm or cool completely and store in an airtight container at room temperature.
Makes 21 mini muffins

Note: To toast and skin hazelnuts, spread them in a single layer in a jelly-roll pan. Bake at 350°F for 10 to 15 minutes, shaking pan a couple of times, until nuts are lightly browned under their skins. Wrap nuts in a clean kitchen towel and cool completely. Place nuts in a sieve and rub them against sieve to remove their skins.

✎ MACADAMIA PAPAYA WHITE CHOCOLATE MINI MUFFINS ✐

Macadamia nuts, white chocolate, and papaya create an irresistible flavor combination.

1 cup all-purpose flour
¼ cup granulated sugar
1¼ teaspoons baking powder
⅛ teaspoon salt
½ cup milk, at room temperature
2 tablespoons vegetable oil
1 large egg (at room temperature), lightly beaten
½ teaspoon vanilla extract

¼ cup chopped dried papaya (see note)
¼ cup white chocolate chips
¼ cup chopped, lightly salted macadamia nuts
24 whole lightly salted macadamia nuts for garnish (optional)

1. Preheat oven to 375°F. Butter twenty-four 1¾ x ¾-inch (about 1-ounce) muffin cups.
2. In a large bowl, stir together flour, sugar, baking powder, and salt. In another bowl, stir together milk, oil, egg, and vanilla. Make a well in center of dry ingredients; add milk mixture and stir just to combine. Stir in papaya, chips, and chopped nuts.
3. Spoon batter into prepared muffin cups. Garnish each muffin with a whole macadamia nut, if desired. Bake for 10 minutes, or until a toothpick inserted in center of one muffin comes out clean.

4. Remove muffin pan(s) to wire rack. Cool for 2 minutes before carefully removing muffins from cups; finish cooling on rack. Serve warm or cool completely and store in an airtight container at room temperature.
Makes 24 mini muffins

Note: Chopped dried pineapple or mango can be substituted for the dried papaya.

Marzipan adds rich almond flavor and a moist dense texture to these little gems.

2 cups all-purpose flour
2 teaspoons baking powder
½ teaspoon salt
1 package (7 ounces) marzipan
¼ cup (½ stick) unsalted butter, softened

¼ cup firmly packed brown sugar
¼ cup granulated sugar
2 large eggs, at room temperature (lightly beaten)
¼ teaspoon almond extract
⅔ cup milk, at room temperature

1. Preheat oven to 400°F. Butter thirty-six 1¾ x ¾-inch (about 1-ounce) muffin cups.
2. In a large bowl, stir together flour, baking powder, and salt. In another large bowl, using a hand-held electric mixer, beat the marzipan, butter, and sugars together until combined. One at a time, add eggs, beating well after each addition. Beat in almond extract. On low speed, in two additions each, add flour mixture and milk.
3. Spoon batter into prepared muffin cups. Bake for 15 to 20 minutes, or until a toothpick inserted in center of one muffin comes out clean.
4. Remove muffin pan(s) to wire rack. Cool for 5 minutes before removing muffins from cups; finish cooling on rack. Serve warm or cool completely and store in an airtight container at room temperature.

These muffins freeze well.

Makes 36 mini muffins

～ PARMESAN PROSCIUTTO MINI MUFFINS ～

These are great as part of the appetizer course. Barb's neighbor, Meg Wittman, suggested this flavor combination. Serve with Parmesan Butter (page 141).

1 cup all-purpose flour
1 cup yellow cornmeal
2 teaspoons granulated sugar
2 teaspoons baking powder
¼ teaspoon salt
¾ cup freshly grated Parmesan
  cheese
1 cup milk, at room temperature

2 large eggs (at room
  temperature), lightly beaten
¼ cup vegetable oil
1 tablespoon Dijon-style mustard
⅛ teaspoon hot pepper sauce
3 ounces finely chopped
  prosciutto (about 1 cup)

1. Preheat oven to 400°F. Butter thirty-six 1¾ x ¾-inch (about 1-ounce) muffin cups.
2. In a large bowl, stir together flour, cornmeal, sugar, baking powder, and salt. Stir in cheese to combine. In another bowl, stir together milk, eggs, oil, mustard, and pepper sauce until blended. Make a well in center of dry ingredients; add milk mixture and stir just to combine. Stir in prosciutto.
3. Spoon batter into prepared muffin cups. Bake for 15 to 20 minutes, or until a toothpick inserted in center of one muffin comes out clean.
4. Remove muffin pans to wire rack. Cool for 5 minutes before carefully removing muffins from cups; finish cooling on rack. Serve warm or cool completely and store in an airtight container in the refrigerator. Let muffins reach room temperature or warm slightly before serving. They are best served warm.
Makes 36 mini muffins

Peanut butter and chocolate, one of America's favorite flavor combinations, create a muffin that's perfect for desserts or snacks.

1 cup all-purpose flour
¼ cup firmly packed dark brown sugar
1½ teaspoons baking powder
⅛ teaspoon salt
⅓ cup peanut butter, at room temperature

1 tablespoon vegetable oil
1 large egg, at room temperature
½ cup milk, at room temperature
½ teaspoon vanilla extract
24 unwrapped milk chocolate kisses

1. Preheat oven to 400°F. Butter twenty-four 1¾ x ¾-inch (about 1-ounce) muffin cups.
2. In a large bowl, stir together flour, sugar, baking powder, and salt. In another bowl, stir together peanut butter and oil. Beat in egg until smooth. Stir in milk and vanilla until blended. Make a well in center of dry ingredients; add milk mixture and stir just to combine.
3. Spoon batter into prepared muffin cups. Bake for 10 minutes, or until a toothpick inserted in center of one muffin comes out clean.
4. Remove muffin pan(s) to wire rack. Cool for 1 minute before carefully removing muffins from cups. Place a chocolate kiss on top of each hot muffin; cool on rack for 30 minutes. Lightly press melted bottoms of chocolate kisses onto muffins. Refrigerate for 1 hour to cool completely. Store in an airtight container at room temperature.

Makes 24 mini muffins

≋ Spiced Pumpkin Mini Muffins ≋

Moist and spicy, these miniature gems are perfect as part of a feast to celebrate the fall. Bring a basket full to a tailgate party, hayrack ride, or Halloween party.

2 cups all-purpose flour
⅔ cup firmly packed light brown sugar
2 teaspoons baking powder
¼ teaspoon baking soda
½ teaspoon salt
1 teaspoon ground cinnamon
¼ teaspoon ground ginger
⅛ teaspoon ground cloves

Dash ground nutmeg
1 cup canned pumpkin
⅓ cup (5⅓ tablespoons) unsalted butter, melted and cooled
2 large eggs (at room temperature), lightly beaten
¼ cup milk, at room temperature
2 teaspoons vanilla extract

1. Preheat oven to 400°F. Butter thirty-six 1¾ x ¾-inch (about 1-ounce) muffin cups.
2. In a large bowl, stir together flour, sugar, baking powder, baking soda, salt, cinnamon, ginger, cloves, and nutmeg. In another bowl, stir together pumpkin, butter, eggs, milk, and vanilla until blended. Make a well in center of dry ingredients; add pumpkin mixture and stir just to combine.
3. Spoon batter into prepared muffin cups. Bake for 15 to 20 minutes, or until a toothpick inserted in center of one muffin comes out clean.
4. Remove muffin pans to wire rack. Cool for 5 minutes before carefully

removing muffins from cups; finish cooling on rack. Serve warm or cool completely and store in an airtight container at room temperature.
These muffins freeze well.
Makes 36 mini muffins

MEGA MUFFINS

✒ BIG MAMMA'S PEANUT BUTTER AND JELLY MUFFINS ✒

This classic comfort flavor combination gains sophistication when topped with a buttery brown sugar topping.

BROWN SUGAR STREUSEL TOPPING

⅓ cup all-purpose flour
3 tablespoons firmly packed light brown sugar

⅛ teaspoon ground cinnamon
3 tablespoons unsalted butter, chilled

PEANUT BUTTER MUFFINS

1¾ cups all-purpose flour
⅔ cup firmly packed light brown sugar
2½ teaspoons baking powder
¼ teaspoon salt
¾ cup milk, at room temperature
⅔ cup smooth or chunky peanut butter

¼ cup vegetable oil
1 large egg, at room temperature
1½ teaspoons vanilla extract
¼ cup favorite flavor of jelly, jam, or preserves

1. Preheat oven to 350°F. Butter six 3¼ x 1⅜-inch (about ⅔-cup) muffin cups and edges surrounding the cups.
2. *To prepare brown sugar streusel topping:* In a small bowl, stir together flour, brown sugar, and cinnamon. Cut butter into ½-inch cubes and dis-

tribute them over flour mixture. Using your fingertips, quickly rub butter into mixture until it resembles coarse crumbs. Set aside.

3. *To prepare peanut butter muffins:* In a large bowl, stir together flour, sugar, baking powder, and salt. In another bowl, stir together milk, peanut butter, oil, egg, and vanilla. Make a well in center of dry ingredients, add milk mixture, and stir just to combine.

4. Spoon about ⅓ cup of batter into each prepared muffin cup. Place 2 teaspoons jelly in center of each portion of batter; do not let jelly touch sides of cups. Spoon remaining batter (about 2 tablespoons per cup) over jelly. Sprinkle streusel topping evenly over tops of muffins. Bake for 25 to 30 minutes, or until lightly browned.

5. Remove muffin pan to wire rack. Cool for 5 minutes before carefully removing muffins from cups; finish cooling on rack. Serve warm or cool completely and store in an airtight container at room temperature.

Makes 6 big mamma muffins

～ BLUEBERRY CHEESE MEGA MUFFINS ～

These decadent king-size muffins, chock-full of blueberry preserves and cheese, are perfect for Sunday brunch or dessert.

CHEESE TOPPING

1 package (3 ounces) cream
  cheese, at room temperature

1 tablespoon granulated sugar
¼ teaspoon vanilla extract

CRUMB TOPPING

¼ cup all-purpose flour
1½ tablespoons firmly packed
  light brown sugar
Generous dash ground cinnamon

Generous dash salt
1½ tablespoons unsalted butter,
  chilled

MUFFINS

1¾ cups all-purpose flour
⅓ cup granulated sugar
2 teaspoons baking powder
¼ teaspoon salt
¾ cup milk, at room temperature
⅓ cup (5⅓ tablespoons) unsalted
  butter, melted and cooled

1 large egg (at room temperature),
  lightly beaten
1 teaspoon vanilla extract
Rounded ⅔ cup blueberry
  preserves (see note)

1. Preheat oven to 400°F. Butter six 3½ x 1¾-inch (about ⅞-cup) muffin cups.

69

2. *To prepare cheese topping:* In a small bowl, stir together cream cheese, granulated sugar, and vanilla until blended. Set aside.

3. *To prepare crumb topping:* In a small bowl, stir together flour, brown sugar, cinnamon, and salt. Cut butter into small cubes and distribute them over flour mixture. With a pastry blender or two knives used scissors fashion, cut in butter until mixture resembles course crumbs. Set aside.

4. *To prepare muffins:* In a large bowl, stir together flour, granulated sugar, baking powder, and salt. In another bowl, stir together milk, butter, egg, and vanilla. Make a well in center of dry ingredients; add milk mixture and stir just to combine.

5. Divide a little less than half of batter among prepared muffin cups, spreading batter to cover bottoms of the cups. Place 1 level tablespoon blueberry preserves in center of each portion of batter; do not let preserves touch sides of cups. Carefully spread with remaining batter, dividing evenly among muffin cups. Top each muffin with 1 heaping teaspoonful cream cheese topping, dividing evenly among muffin cups. Top each muffin with 2 teaspoons blueberry preserves. Sprinkle crumb topping evenly over tops of muffins. Bake for 20 to 25 minutes, or until lightly browned.

6. Remove muffin pan to wire rack. Cool for 10 minutes before carefully removing muffins from cups; finish cooling on rack. Serve warm or cool completely and store in an airtight container in the refrigerator. Let muffins reach room temperature before serving.

Makes 6 mega muffins

Note: Blueberry pie filling can be used in place of the preserves. Top each muffin with 1 tablespoon pie filling.

These super-rich, super-size muffins topped with cherry pie filling are perfect for teatime, snacks, and desserts.

STREUSEL FILLING/TOPPING

⅓ cup all-purpose flour
3 tablespoons ground almonds
2 tablespoons firmly packed light
   brown sugar

⅛ teaspoon ground cinnamon
Generous dash salt
2 tablespoons unsalted butter,
   chilled

MUFFINS

1¾ cups all-purpose flour
⅓ cup granulated sugar
2 teaspoons baking powder
¼ teaspoon salt
¾ cup milk, at room temperature
⅓ cup (5⅓ tablespoons) unsalted
   butter, melted and cooled

1 large egg (at room temperature),
   lightly beaten
1 teaspoon vanilla extract
¼ teaspoon almond extract
Approximately ¾ cup cherry pie
   filling

1. Preheat oven to 400°F. Butter six 3½ x 1¾-inch (about ⅞-cup) muffin cups.
2. *To prepare streusel filling/topping:* In a small bowl, stir together flour, nuts, brown sugar, cinnamon, and salt. Cut butter into ½-inch cubes and distribute them over flour mixture. With a pastry blender or two knives used scissors fashion, cut in butter until mixture resembles coarse crumbs. Set aside.

3. *To prepare muffins:* In a large bowl, stir together flour, granulated sugar, baking powder, and salt. In another bowl, stir together milk, butter, egg, vanilla, and almond extracts. Make a well in center of dry ingredients; add milk mixture and stir just to combine.

4. Divide a little less than half of the batter among prepared muffin cups, spreading batter to cover bottoms of the cups. Place 1 level tablespoon cherry pie filling in center of each portion of batter, using three cherries; do not let filling touch sides of cups. Set aside ½ cup streusel filling/topping. Sprinkle remaining streusel filling/topping evenly over muffins. Carefully spread muffins with remaining batter, dividing evenly among muffin cups. Top each muffin with 1 level tablespoon cherry pie filling. Sprinkle remaining streusel filling/topping evenly over tops of muffins. Bake for 20 to 25 minutes, or until lightly browned.

5. Remove muffin pans to wire rack. Cool for 10 minutes before carefully removing muffins from cups; finish cooling on rack. Serve warm or cool completely and store in an airtight container in the refrigerator. Let muffins reach room temperature before serving.

Makes 6 mega muffins

Make sure not to over-blend these two batters so you have definite marble-izing throughout the muffins

1 ounce semisweet chocolate
2 cups all-purpose flour
½ cup granulated sugar
2 teaspoons baking powder
¼ teaspoon salt
¾ cup milk, at room temperature

½ cup (1 stick) unsalted butter, melted and cooled
2 large eggs (at room temperature), lightly beaten
2 teaspoons vanilla extract
1 cup semisweet chocolate chips

1. Preheat oven to 400°F. Butter six 3¼ x 1⅜-inch (about ⅔-cup) muffin cups and edges surrounding the cups.
2. In a microwave-safe bowl, heat semisweet chocolate in a microwave oven on High for 1 to 2 minutes, stirring halfway through cooking, until melted (or use a double boiler over hot, not simmering water). Cool mixture at room temperature for 10 minutes.
3. In a large bowl, stir together flour, sugar, baking powder, and salt. In another bowl, stir together milk, butter, eggs, and vanilla. Make a well in center of dry ingredients; add milk mixture and stir just to combine.
4. Remove ⅔ cup of batter and stir in melted chocolate until just combined. Stir chips into plain batter. Using a rubber spatula, lightly fold the two batters together so they are swirled, but not blended.
5. Spoon batter into prepared muffin cups. Bake for 25 to 30 minutes, or until a toothpick inserted in center of one muffin comes out clean.

6. Remove muffin pan to wire rack. Cool for 10 minutes before carefully removing muffins from cups; finish cooling on rack. Serve warm or cool completely and store in an airtight container at room temperature.

These muffins freeze well.

Makes 6 mega muffins

While this muffin is big enough to share, you won't want to! Melting-ly delicious chunks of bittersweet chocolate are enveloped in a big rich muffin.

2 cups all-purpose flour
⅓ cup firmly packed light brown sugar
⅓ cup granulated sugar
2 teaspoons baking powder
½ teaspoon salt
⅔ cup milk, at room temperature
½ cup (1 stick) unsalted butter, melted and cooled

2 large eggs (at room temperature), lightly beaten
2 teaspoons vanilla extract
12 ounces bittersweet chocolate, cut into chunks
⅓ cup coarsely broken walnuts or pecans

1. Preheat oven to 400°F. Butter six 3¼ x 1⅜-inch (about ⅔-cup) muffin cups and edges surrounding the cups.
2. In a large bowl, stir together flour, sugars, baking powder, and salt. In another bowl, stir together milk, butter, eggs, and vanilla until blended. Make a well in center of dry ingredients; add milk mixture and stir just to combine. Stir in chocolate chunks and nuts.
3. Spoon batter into prepared muffin cups. Bake for 25 to 30 minutes, or until a toothpick inserted in center of one muffin comes out clean.
4. Remove muffin pan to wire rack. Cool for 10 minutes before carefully

removing muffins from cups; finish cooling on rack. Serve warm or cool completely and store in an airtight container at room temperature.
These muffins freeze well.
Makes 6 jumbo muffins

Pineapple upside-down cake in the form of a muffin—rich enough to be served for dessert.

TOPPING

2 tablespoons unsalted
butter
⅓ cup firmly packed light brown
sugar

6 canned pineapple slices packed
in juice, well drained (reserve
juice from 20-ounce can)
12 dried tart cherries or 24 raisins

MUFFINS

1½ cups all-purpose flour
¼ cup firmly packed light brown
sugar
1½ teaspoons baking powder
¼ teaspoon salt
⅔ cup pineapple juice

¼ cup (½ stick) unsalted butter,
melted and cooled
1 large egg (at room temperature),
lightly beaten
1 teaspoon vanilla extract

1. Preheat oven to 400°F. Butter six 3½ x 1¾-inch (about ⅞-cup) muffin cups
   and edges surrounding the cups.
2. *To prepare topping:* In a small saucepan, melt butter over low heat. Stir in
   sugar. Cook, stirring, for 1½ minutes. Divide butter mixture among muffin
   cups, spreading to coat bottoms of the cups. Place a pineapple slice in
   each muffin cup, pressing it into bottom to fit. Place 2 dried cherries or
   4 raisins in center of each pineapple slice. Set aside.

3. *To prepare muffins:* In a large bowl, stir together flour, sugar, baking powder, and salt. In another bowl, stir together juice, butter, egg, and vanilla Make a well in center of dry ingredients; add juice mixture and stir just to combine.
4. Spoon batter into prepared muffin cups. Bake for 15 to 20 minutes or until a toothpick inserted in center of one muffin comes out clean.
5. Remove muffin pan to wire rack. Cool for 10 minutes before carefully removing muffins from cups by running a spatula around edges and inverting onto serving platter. Serve warm or cool completely and store in an airtight container in the refrigerator. Let muffins reach room temperature or warm slightly before serving. These muffins are best served warm.

Makes 6 mega muffins

Note: To reheat these muffins, place in a small microwave-safe bowl. Cover and heat in a microwave oven on Medium for 30 to 60 seconds, or until heated through.

Be sure to make these muffins in the spring and summer when strawberries and rhubarb are readily available.

STREUSEL TOPPING

3 tablespoons all-purpose flour
1 tablespoon firmly packed light
  brown sugar
Generous dash ground cinnamon
Generous dash salt

1 tablespoon unsalted butter,
  chilled
2 tablespoons finely chopped
  walnuts

MUFFINS

1¾ cups all-purpose flour
2 teaspoons baking powder
½ teaspoon ground cinnamon
¼ teaspoon salt
¾ cup granulated sugar
⅓ cup (5⅓ tablespoons) unsalted
  butter, at room temperature

1 large egg (at room temperature),
  lightly beaten
1 teaspoon vanilla extract
1 cup diced rhubarb
1 cup diced strawberries

1. Preheat oven to 400°F. Butter six 3½ x 1¾-inch (about ⅞-cup) muffin cups.
2. *To prepare streusel topping:* In a small bowl, stir together flour, brown sugar, cinnamon, and salt. Cut butter into small cubes and distribute them over flour mixture. With a pastry blender or two knives used scissors fashion, cut in butter until mixture resembles coarse crumbs. Stir in nuts. Set aside.

3. *To prepare muffins:* In a small bowl, stir together flour, baking powder, cinnamon, and salt. In a large bowl, and using a hand-held electric mixer, cream together granulated sugar and butter for 2 minutes, or until light. Beat in egg and vanilla until blended. Stir in flour mixture just to combine. The batter will be stiff. Stir in rhubarb and strawberries.
4. Spoon batter into prepared muffin cups. Sprinkle streusel topping evenly over tops of muffins. Bake for 25 to 30 minutes, or until a toothpick inserted in center of one muffin comes out clean.
5. Remove muffin pan to wire rack. Cool for 10 minutes before carefully removing muffins from cups; finish cooling on rack. Serve warm or cool completely and store in an airtight container in the refrigerator. Let muffins reach room temperature before serving.

Makes 6 mega muffins

❧ Texas-Size Big Bran Muffins ❧

Chopped dates add moistness and sweetness to these big bran muffins. For a desk-top lunch, add a container of yogurt and a piece of fresh fruit.

1½ cups bran cereal (such as
   100% Bran)
1 cup buttermilk, at room
   temperature
2 large eggs (at room
   temperature), lightly beaten
¼ cup (½ stick) butter, melted and
   cooled
3 tablespoons vegetable oil

2 tablespoons molasses
1 teaspoon vanilla extract
¼ cup firmly packed brown sugar
1 cup all-purpose flour
1½ teaspoons baking powder
½ teaspoon baking soda
¼ teaspoon salt
1 cup chopped pitted dates

1. Preheat oven to 375°F. Butter six 3¼ x 1⅜-inch (about ⅔-cup) muffin cups and edges surrounding the cups.
2. In a large bowl, stir together bran cereal and buttermilk. Let stand for about 5 minutes, or until buttermilk is absorbed. In another bowl, stir together eggs, butter, oil, molasses, and vanilla until blended. Stir in sugar, then the bran mixture. In another large bowl, stir together flour, baking powder, baking soda, and salt. Make a well in center of dry ingredients; add bran mixture and stir just to combine. Stir in dates.
3. Spoon batter into prepared muffin cups. Bake for 15 to 20 minutes, or until a toothpick inserted in center of one muffin comes out clean.
4. Remove muffin pan. Cool for 5 minutes before carefully removing muffins

from cups; finish cooling on rack. Serve warm or cool completely and store in an airtight container at room temperature.

These muffins freeze well.

Makes 6 big muffins

❧ SOMEWHAT HEALTHIER MUFFINS ❧

Almonds add crunch to these tangy apricot muffins. They're delicious spread with Neufchâtel cheese.

1¾ cups all-purpose flour
⅔ cup firmly packed light brown sugar
1 teaspoon baking powder
1 teaspoon baking soda
¼ teaspoon salt
1 cup fat-free buttermilk, at room temperature

2 large egg whites (at room temperature), lightly beaten
2 tablespoons canola oil
1 teaspoon vanilla extract
¼ teaspoon almond extract
⅓ cup chopped dried apricots
⅓ cup chopped toasted slivered almonds (see note)

1. Preheat oven to 400°F. Lightly coat twelve 3 x 1¼-inch (3½- to 4-ounce) muffin cups and edges surrounding the cups with nonstick vegetable cooking spray.
2. In a large bowl, stir together flour, sugar, baking powder, baking soda, and salt. In another bowl, stir together buttermilk, egg whites, oil, vanilla, and almond extracts. Make a well in center of dry ingredients; add milk mixture and stir just to combine. Stir in apricots and nuts.
3. Spoon batter into prepared muffin cups. Bake for 15 to 20 minutes, or until a toothpick inserted in center of one muffin comes out clean.
4. Remove muffin pan(s) to wire rack. Cool for 5 minutes before carefully removing muffins from cups; finish cooling on rack. Serve warm or cool completely and store in an airtight container at room temperature.

Makes 12 muffins

Note: To toast almonds, place them in a single layer in a jelly-roll pan or on a baking sheet and bake at 350°F for 5 to 7 minutes, shaking sheet a couple of times, until nuts are lightly browned.

Nutrition information per muffin:

- 154 calories
- 25 grams carbohydrate
- 4 grams protein
- 5 grams fat
- 1 milligram cholesterol
- 225 milligrams sodium

These moist muffins are packed with flavor because of grated carrot and crushed pineapple. They freeze well. Keep them on hand and pop them into a lunch box in the morning for a flavorful and low-fat treat.

1 cup whole wheat flour
1 cup uncooked old-fashioned
   rolled oats
1½ teaspoons baking powder
½ teaspoon baking soda
¼ teaspoon salt
½ teaspoon ground cinnamon
Dash ground ginger
Dash ground cloves
Dash ground nutmeg
½ cup crushed pineapple in
   unsweetened juice

⅓ cup plain nonfat yogurt, at
   room temperature
2 large egg whites (at room
   temperature), lightly beaten
2 tablespoons canola oil
2 teaspoons vanilla extract
½ cup firmly packed light brown
   sugar
1½ cups shredded carrots
½ cup golden raisins
Confectioners' sugar for dusting
   tops of muffins (optional)

1. Preheat oven to 400°F. Lightly coat nine 3 x 1¼-inch (3½- to 4-ounce) muffin cups with nonstick vegetable cooking spray.
2. In a large bowl, stir together flour, oats, baking powder, baking soda, salt, cinnamon, ginger, cloves, and nutmeg. In another bowl, stir together pineapple, yogurt, egg whites, oil, and vanilla. Stir in brown sugar until blended. Make a well in center of dry ingredients; add pineapple mixture and stir just to combine. Stir in carrots and raisins.

3. Spoon batter into prepared muffin cups. Bake for 17 to 19 minutes, or until a toothpick inserted in center of one muffin comes out clean.
4. Remove muffin pan(s) to wire rack. Cool for 5 minutes before carefully removing muffins from cups; finish cooling on rack. Sift confectioners' sugar over tops of cooled muffins, if desired. Serve warm or cool completely and store in an airtight container at cool room temperature.

These muffins freeze well.

Makes 9 muffins

Nutrition information per muffin:

- 191   calories
- 35   grams carbohydrate
- 5   grams protein
- 4   grams fat
    Trace cholesterol
- 240   milligrams sodium

These muffins have a rich deep chocolate flavor that comes from cocoa powder. A light dusting of confectioners' sugar adds a pretty touch to the tops of these muffins.

1¾ cups all-purpose flour
⅔ cup granulated sugar
½ cup unsweetened nonalkalized cocoa powder
2 teaspoons baking powder
¼ teaspoon baking soda
¼ teaspoon salt

1¼ cups fat-free buttermilk, at room temperature
¼ cup canola oil
2 large egg whites (at room temperature), lightly beaten
1½ teaspoons vanilla extract
1 tablespoon confectioners' sugar

1. Preheat oven to 375°F. Lightly coat twelve 2⅝-inch x 1⅛-inch (about 3-ounce) muffin cups with nonstick vegetable cooking spray.
2. In a large bowl, stir together flour, sugar, cocoa powder, baking powder, baking soda, and salt. In another bowl, stir together buttermilk, oil, egg whites, and vanilla until blended. Make a well in center of dry ingredients; add milk mixture and stir just to combine.
3. Spoon batter into prepared muffin cups. Bake for 15 to 20 minutes, or until a toothpick inserted in center of one muffin comes out clean.
4. Remove muffin pan(s) to wire rack. Cool for 5 minutes before removing muffins from cups; finish cooling on rack. Sift confectioners' sugar over tops of cooled muffins. Serve warm or cool completely and store in an airtight container at room temperature.

Makes 12 muffins

Nutrition information per muffin:

175 calories
29 grams carbohydrate
4 grams protein
5 grams fat
Trace cholesterol
189 milligrams sodium

If you are looking to get a healthy dose of oat bran, these muffins are all oat bran—no flour.

2 cups oat bran
2 teaspoons baking powder
½ teaspoon baking soda
⅛ teaspoon salt
⅔ cup plain nonfat yogurt, at room temperature
¼ cup orange juice, at room temperature
2 large egg whites (at room temperature), lightly beaten

2 tablespoons canola oil
1 teaspoon vanilla extract
¼ teaspoon grated orange peel
½ cup firmly packed light brown sugar
1 cup chopped fresh or frozen cranberries
1 tablespoon granulated sugar

1. Preheat oven to 400°F. Lightly coat thirty 1¾ x ⅞-inch (about 1-ounce) muffin cups with nonstick vegetable cooking spray.
2. In a large bowl, stir together oat bran, baking powder, baking soda, and salt. In another bowl, stir together yogurt, orange juice, egg whites, oil, vanilla, and orange peel. Stir in brown sugar until combined. Make a well in center of dry ingredients; add yogurt mixture and stir just to combine. In a small bowl, stir together cranberries and granulated sugar to combine. Stir cranberries into batter.
3. Spoon batter into prepared muffin cups. Bake for 15 to 17 minutes, or until a toothpick inserted in center of one muffin comes out clean.

3. Remove muffin pans to wire rack. Cool for 5 minutes before carefully removing muffins from cups; finish cooling on rack. Serve warm or cool completely and store in an airtight container at room temperature.

These muffins freeze well.

Makes 30 mini muffins

Nutrition information per muffin:

- 41 calories
- 8 grams carbohydrate
- 1 gram protein
- 1 gram fat
   Trace cholesterol
- 71 milligrams sodium

❧ Date Nut Oat Bran Muffins ❧

A hint of orange peel brightens up these hearty muffins.

1 cup fat-free milk	¼ teaspoon salt
1½ cups chopped pitted dates	2 large egg whites (at room
1⅓ cups oat bran	temperature), lightly beaten
⅔ cup all-purpose flour	3 tablespoons canola oil
3 tablespoons firmly packed light	½ teaspoon vanilla extract
brown sugar	⅛ teaspoon grated orange peel
1 tablespoon baking powder	¼ cup chopped walnuts

1. Preheat oven to 375°F. Lightly coat twelve 2⅝-inch x 1⅛-inch (about 3-ounce) muffins cups with nonstick vegetable cooking spray.
2. In a 1-quart saucepan, scald milk over medium heat. Stir in dates and let stand for 20 minutes.
3. In a large bowl, stir together oat bran, flour, sugar, baking powder, and salt. In another bowl, stir together egg whites, oil, vanilla, and orange peel. Make a well in center of dry ingredients; add egg white mixture and stir just to combine. Stir in date mixture and nuts.
4. Spoon batter into prepared muffin cups. Bake for 18 to 23 minutes, or until a toothpick inserted in center of one muffin comes out clean.
5. Remove muffin pan(s) to wire rack. Cool for 5 minutes before carefully removing muffins from cups; finish cooling on rack. Serve warm or cool completely and store in an airtight container at room temperature.
Makes 12 muffins

Nutrition information per muffin:

- 175 calories
- 32 grams carbohydrate
- 5 grams protein
- 6 grams fat
  Trace cholesterol
- 188 milligrams sodium

Ginger is a natural with sweet potatoes, and these muffins have it two ways, using both ground and crystallized candied ginger. Try them with the Candied Ginger Butter (page 138).

1¾ cups all-purpose flour
¾ cup firmly packed light brown
  sugar
2 teaspoons baking powder
¼ teaspoon baking soda
¼ teaspoon salt
½ teaspoon ground cinnamon
¼ teaspoon ground ginger
¾ cup mashed baked sweet
  potato, cooled

½ cup fat-free milk, at room
  temperature
2 large eggs (at room
  temperature), lightly beaten
3 tablespoons canola oil
1½ teaspoons vanilla extract
¼ to ⅓ cup finely chopped
  crystallized ginger

1. Preheat oven to 375°F. Lightly coat twelve 2⅝-inch x 1⅛-inch (about 3-ounce) muffin cups with nonstick vegetable cooking spray.
2. In a large bowl, stir together flour, sugar, baking powder, baking soda, salt, cinnamon, and ground ginger. In another bowl, stir together sweet potato, milk, eggs, oil, and vanilla until blended. Make a well in center of dry ingredients; add milk mixture and stir just to combine. Stir in crystallized ginger.
3. Spoon batter into prepared muffin cups. Bake for 15 to 20 minutes, or until a toothpick inserted in center of one muffin comes out clean.

4. Remove muffin pan(s) to wire rack. Cool for 5 minutes before removing muffins from cups; finish cooling on rack. Serve warm or cool completely and store in an airtight container at room temperature.

Makes 12 muffins

Nutrition information per muffin:

168	calories
28	grams carbohydrate
3	grams protein
4	grams fat
35	milligrams cholesterol
173	milligrams sodium

An easy-to-prepare muffin that goes well with meals or snacks.

1½ cups whole wheat flour
½ cup all-purpose flour
¼ cup granulated sugar
1 teaspoon baking powder
1 teaspoon baking soda
¼ teaspoon salt
1 container (8 ounces) plain
  nonfat yogurt (about 1 cup),
  at room temperature

2 large egg whites (at room
  temperature), lightly beaten
⅓ cup honey
2 tablespoons canola oil
1 teaspoon vanilla extract
⅔ cup raisins

1. Preheat oven to 400°F. Lightly coat twelve 2½ x 1-inch (2- to 2½-ounce) muffin cups with nonstick vegetable cooking spray.
2. In a large bowl, stir together flours, sugar, baking powder, baking soda, and salt. In another bowl, stir together yogurt, egg whites, honey, oil, and vanilla. Make a well in center of dry ingredients; add yogurt mixture and stir just to combine. Stir in raisins.
3. Spoon batter into prepared muffin cups. Bake for 15 to 20 minutes, or until a toothpick inserted in center of one muffin comes out clean.
4. Remove muffin pan(s) to wire rack. Cool for 5 minutes before carefully removing muffins from cups. Serve warm or cool completely and store in an airtight container at room temperature.

Makes 12 muffins

Nutrition information per muffin:

171   calories
 33   grams carbohydrate
  5   grams protein
  3   grams fat
     Trace cholesterol
216   milligrams sodium

The creamy cheese filling is the perfect complement for this tangy muffin.

CHEESE TOPPING

3 ounces Neufchâtel cheese, at room temperature

2 tablespoons granulated sugar
½ teaspoon vanilla extract

LEMON MUFFINS

2 cups all-purpose flour
⅔ cup granulated sugar
2½ teaspoons baking powder
¼ teaspoon salt
1 cup fat-free milk, at room temperature

2 large egg whites (lightly beaten), at room temperature
2 tablespoons canola oil
1¼ teaspoons grated lemon peel
1 teaspoon vanilla extract

1. Preheat oven to 400°F. Lightly coat twelve 3 x 1¼-inch (3½- to 4-ounce) muffin cups with nonstick vegetable cooking spray.
2. *To prepare topping:* In a small bowl, stir together cheese, 1 tablespoon of the sugar, and vanilla until blended. Set aside.
3. *To prepare muffins:* In a large bowl, stir together flour, sugar, baking powder, and salt. In another bowl, stir together milk, egg whites, oil, lemon peel, and vanilla. Make a well in center of dry ingredients; add milk mixture and stir just to combine.
4. Spoon batter into prepared muffin cups. Top each muffin with 1 rounded teaspoonful cheese topping, dividing evenly among the muffin cups.

Sprinkle remaining tablespoon sugar evenly over tops of muffins. Bake for 15 to 20 minutes, or until a toothpick inserted in center of one muffin comes out clean.

5. Remove muffin pan(s) to wire rack. Cool for 5 minutes before carefully removing muffins from cups. Serve warm or cool completely and store in an airtight container in the refrigerator. Let muffins reach room temperature before serving.

Makes 12 muffins

Nutrition information per muffin:

170	calories
29	grams carbohydrate
4	grams protein
4	grams fat
5	milligrams cholesterol
197	milligrams sodium

✒ Banana Oat Bran Mini Muffins ✒

These flavorful muffins will delight every banana lover, without a lot of fat.

1 cup oat bran
1 cup all-purpose flour
¼ cup granulated sugar
¼ cup firmly packed brown sugar
1½ teaspoons baking powder
¼ teaspoon salt
⅔ cup mashed ripe banana (about 1 large)

½ cup plain nonfat yogurt, at room temperature
¼ cup canola oil
2 large egg whites (at room temperature), lightly beaten
1½ teaspoons vanilla extract
¼ cup chopped walnuts (optional)

1. Preheat oven to 375°F. Lightly coat twenty-four 1¾ x ⅞-inch (about 1-ounce) muffin cups with nonstick vegetable cooking spray.
2. In a large bowl, stir together oat bran, flour, sugars, baking powder, and salt. In another bowl, stir together banana, yogurt, oil, egg whites, and vanilla. Make a well in center of dry ingredients; add banana mixture and stir just to combine. Stir in nuts, if desired.
3. Spoon batter into prepared muffin cups. Bake for 15 to 17 minutes, or until a toothpick inserted in center of one muffin comes out clean.
4. Remove muffin pans to wire rack. Cool for 5 minutes before carefully removing muffins from cups; finish cooling on rack. Serve warm or cool completely and store in an airtight container at room temperature.

These muffins freeze well.

Makes 24 mini muffins

Nutrition information per muffin (without walnuts):

- 71 calories
- 12 grams carbohydrate
- 2 grams protein
- 2 grams fat
  Trace cholesterol
- 62 milligrams sodium

≈ OATMEAL RAISIN MUFFINS ≈
(ON THE LIGHTER SIDE)

Reminiscent of old-fashioned oatmeal raisin cookies, these muffins go well with a container of yogurt.

1 cup all-purpose flour
1 cup uncooked old-fashioned rolled oats
½ cup firmly packed light brown sugar
2½ teaspoons baking powder
¼ teaspoon salt

½ cup fat-free milk, at room temperature
2 large egg whites (at room temperature), lightly beaten
2 tablespoons canola oil
1½ teaspoons vanilla extract
¾ cup raisins

1. Preheat oven to 400°F. Lightly coat eight 2⅝-inch x 1⅛-inch (about 3-ounce) muffin cups with nonstick vegetable cooking spray.
2. In a large bowl, stir together flour, oats, sugar, baking powder, and salt. In another bowl, stir together milk, egg whites, oil, and vanilla until blended. Make a well in center of dry ingredients; add milk mixture and stir just to combine. Stir in raisins.
3. Spoon batter into prepared muffin cups. Bake for 15 to 20 minutes, or until a toothpick inserted in center of one muffin comes out clean.
4. Remove muffin pan(s) to wire rack. Cool for 5 minutes before carefully removing muffins from cups; finish cooling on rack. Serve warm or cool completely and store in an airtight container at room temperature.

These muffins freeze well.

Makes 8 muffins

Nutrition information per muffin:

208 calories
39 grams carbohydrate
5 grams protein
4 grams fat
Trace cholesterol
246 milligrams sodium

The tangy combination of orange and pineapple create muffins that are high in flavor, but low in fat.

1¾ cups all-purpose flour
⅔ cup firmly packed light brown sugar
1 teaspoon baking powder
1 teaspoon baking soda
¼ teaspoon salt
1 can (8 ounces) crushed pineapple in juice

⅓ cup fat-free milk, at room temperature
2 large egg whites (lightly beaten), at room temperature
2 tablespoons canola oil
1 teaspoon grated orange peel
1 teaspoon vanilla extract
⅓ cup sweetened flaked coconut

1. Preheat oven to 400°F. Lightly coat twelve 3 x 1¼-inch (3½- to 4-ounce) muffin cups with nonstick vegetable cooking spray.

2. In a large bowl, stir together flour, sugar, baking powder, baking soda, and salt. In another bowl, stir together pineapple in juice, milk, egg whites, oil, orange peel, and vanilla. Make a well in center of dry ingredients; add milk mixture and stir just to combine.

3. Spoon batter into prepared muffin cups. Sprinkle coconut evenly over tops of muffins. Bake for 10 to 15 minutes, or until a toothpick inserted in center of one muffin comes out clean.

4. Remove muffin pan(s) to wire rack. Cool for 5 minutes before carefully removing muffins from cups; finish cooling on rack. Serve warm or cool completely and store in an airtight container at room temperature.

Makes 12 muffins

Nutrition information per muffin:

137   calories
 24   grams carbohydrate
  3   grams protein
  3   grams fat
     Trace cholesterol
211   milligrams sodium

❧ ORANGE POPPY SEED MUFFINS ❧

This tangy muffin is perfect for breakfast or a quick snack.

1¾ cups all-purpose flour
⅔ cup firmly packed light brown sugar
2 tablespoons poppy seeds
1 teaspoon baking powder
1 teaspoon baking soda
¼ teaspoon salt

1 cup fat-free buttermilk, at room temperature
2 large egg whites (lightly beaten), at room temperature
2 tablespoons canola oil
1¼ teaspoons grated orange peel
1 teaspoon vanilla extract

1. Preheat oven to 400°F. Lightly coat twelve 2½ x 1-inch (2- to 2½-ounce) muffin cups with nonstick vegetable cooking spray.
2. In a large bowl, stir together flour, sugar, poppy seeds, baking powder, baking soda, and salt. In another bowl, stir together buttermilk, egg whites, oil, orange peel, and vanilla. Make a well in center of dry ingredients; add milk mixture and stir just to combine.
3. Spoon batter into prepared muffin cups. Bake for 10 to 15 minutes, or until a toothpick inserted in center of one muffin comes out clean.
4. Remove muffin pan(s) to wire rack. Cool for 5 minutes before carefully removing muffins from cups; finish cooling on rack. Serve warm or cool completely and store in an airtight container at room temperature.

Makes 12 muffins

Nutrition information per muffin:

- 131 calories
- 22 grams carbohydrate
- 3 grams protein
- 3 grams fat
- 1 milligram cholesterol
- 224 milligrams sodium

≈ SPICED CHUNKY APPLESAUCE MUFFINS ≈

Using applesauce for moistness allows these tender muffins to be made with only 2 tablespoons of oil.

2 cups all-purpose flour
¾ cup firmly packed light brown sugar
2½ teaspoons baking powder
¼ teaspoon salt
1 teaspoon ground cinnamon
⅛ teaspoon ground nutmeg
⅛ teaspoon ground cloves

⅛ teaspoon ground ginger
¾ cup chunky applesauce, at room temperature
½ cup fat-free milk
2 large egg whites (at room temperature), lightly beaten
2 tablespoons canola oil
¾ cup raisins

1. Preheat oven to 400°F. Lightly coat twelve 2⅜ x 1⅛-inch (about 3-ounce) muffin cups with nonstick vegetable cooking spray.
2. In a large bowl, stir together flour, sugar, baking powder, salt, cinnamon, nutmeg, cloves, and ginger. In another bowl, stir together applesauce, milk, egg whites, and oil until blended. Make a well in center of dry ingredients; add applesauce mixture and stir just to combine. Stir in raisins.
3. Spoon batter into prepared muffin cups. Bake for 20 to 25 minutes, or until a toothpick inserted in center of one muffin comes out clean.
4. Remove muffin pan(s) to wire rack. Cool for 5 minutes before carefully removing muffins from cups; finish cooling on rack. Serve warm or cool completely and store in an airtight container at cool room temperature.

These muffins freeze well.

Makes 12 muffins

Nutrition information per muffin:

- 175 calories
- 36 grams carbohydrate
- 3 grams protein
- 3 grams fat
  Trace cholesterol
- 166 milligrams sodium

These dense round brownies are great served on a plate along with a scoop
of ice cream and a topping of chocolate sauce.

½ cup (1 stick) unsalted butter
2 ounces unsweetened chocolate,
  broken into pieces
1 ounce semisweet chocolate,
  broken into pieces
2 large eggs, at room temperature
½ cup granulated sugar
¼ cup firmly packed light brown
  sugar

1½ teaspoons vanilla extract
½ cup all-purpose flour
⅛ teaspoon salt
¾ cups semisweet chocolate chips
½ cup chopped walnuts or pecans
  (optional)

1. Preheat oven to 350°F. Butter six 3¼ x 1⅜-inch (about ⅔-cup) muffin cups
   and edges surrounding the cups.
2. In a large microwave-safe bowl, heat butter and chocolates in a
   microwave oven on High for 1 to 2 minutes, stirring halfway through
   cooking, until chocolate is melted (or use a double boiler over hot, not
   simmering, water). Cool mixture at room temperature for 20 minutes.
3. In a large bowl, using a hand-held electric mixer set at medium-high
   speed, beat eggs and sugars for 2 to 3 minutes, or until mixture is light in
   color. Beat in chocolate mixture and vanilla until blended. Beat in flour
   and salt just until combined. Using a wooden spoon, stir in chips and nuts,
   if desired.

4. Spoon batter into prepared muffin cups. Bake for 25 to 30 minutes, or until a toothpick inserted in center of one muf-fun comes out clean.
5. Remove muffin pan to wire rack. Cool 5 minutes before removing muf-funs from cups; finish cooling on rack. Serve each muf-fun with a scoop of ice cream and chocolate sauce.

Makes 6 muf-funs

Some people eat only the tops off muffins. Here's the solution—bottomless tops! Use dried cherries and chocolate chips, or your favorite mix-ins.

2 cups all-purpose flour
½ cup firmly packed light brown sugar
1½ teaspoons baking powder
¼ teaspoon baking soda
¼ teaspoon salt
½ cup buttermilk, at room temperature

¼ cup (½ stick) unsalted butter, melted and cooled
1 large egg (at room temperature), lightly beaten
2 teaspoons vanilla extract
½ cup semisweet chocolate chips
⅓ cup dried cherries

1. Preheat oven to 400°F. Butter a baking sheet.
2. In a large bowl, stir together flour, sugar, baking powder, baking soda, and salt. In another bowl, stir together buttermilk, butter, egg, and vanilla until blended. Make a well in center of dry ingredients; add buttermilk mixture and stir just to combine. Stir in chips and cherries.
3. Using a ⅓-cup measuring cup, drop the batter onto prepared baking sheet, leaving about 2 inches between muf-fun tops. Bake for 15 to 20 minutes, or until the tops are lightly browned and a cake tester or toothpick inserted into the center of one muf-fun top comes out clean.
4. Remove baking sheet to wire rack and cool for 5 minutes. Using a spatula, transfer the tops to wire rack to cool. Serve warm, or cool completely and store in an airtight container.

Makes 9 muf-fun tops

Here is a jumbo muffin that is baked in a pie plate. You'll want to share it with a group. Serve a wedge on a plate with a scoop of ice cream.

2 cups all-purpose flour
⅓ cup firmly packed brown sugar
⅓ cup granulated sugar
2 teaspoons baking powder
½ teaspoon salt
½ cup milk, at room temperature
⅓ cup (5⅓ tablespoons) unsalted butter, melted and cooled

2 large eggs (at room temperature) lightly beaten
2 teaspoons vanilla extract
1½ cups semisweet, milk, and/or white chocolate chips
½ cup coarsely broken walnuts or pecans

1. Preheat oven to 350°F. Butter a 9-inch pie plate.
2. In a large bowl, stir together flour, sugars, baking powder, and salt. In another bowl, stir together milk, butter, eggs, and vanilla until blended. Make a well in center of dry ingredients; add milk mixture and stir just to combine. Stir in chips and nuts.
3. Spoon batter into prepared pan. Bake for 25 to 30 minutes, or until a toothpick inserted in center comes out clean.
4. Remove pan to wire rack. Cool for 5 minutes before removing muf-fun from pan; finish cooling on rack. Serve warm or cool completely and store in an airtight container at room temperature.

Makes 1 very big muf-fun; 8 servings

A cross between cinnamon buns and muffins, these rich treats are delicious for breakfast, brunch, or snacks whether they are served plain or with butter. Leslie's nine-year-old daughter Lauren says that kids will like these better without the yucky nuts.

CINNAMON FILLING

1½ tablespoons firmly packed
    light brown sugar
¼ teaspoon ground cinnamon

¼ cup raisins
¼ cup chopped pecans (optional)

MUF-BUNS

1¾ cups all-purpose flour
¼ cup granulated sugar
1½ teaspoons baking powder
¼ teaspoon salt
¼ teaspoon ground cinnamon
¼ cup (½ stick) unsalted butter,
    chilled

⅓ cup milk, at room temperature
1 large egg (at room temperature),
    lightly beaten
1 teaspoon vanilla extract
1 tablespoon unsalted butter,
    melted and cooled

GLAZE

⅓ cup confectioners' sugar
1½ teaspoons water or orange
    juice or more as needed

117

1. Preheat oven to 400°F. Butter six 3½ x 1¾-inch (about ¾-cup) muffin cups.
2. *To prepare filling:* In a small bowl, stir together brown sugar, cinnamon, raisins, and nuts, if desired. Set aside.
3. *To prepare muf-buns:* In a large bowl, stir together flour, granulated sugar, baking powder, salt, and cinnamon. Cut chilled butter into ½-inch cubes and distribute them over flour mixture. With a pastry blender or two knives used scissors fashion, cut in butter until mixture resembles coarse crumbs. In a small bowl, stir together milk, egg, and vanilla. Add milk mixture to flour mixture and stir until combined.
4. With lightly floured hands, pat the dough to an 8 x 10-inch rectangle on a lightly floured cutting board. Brush surface with melted butter. Sprinkle with cinnamon filling. Starting at 8-inch end, roll up jelly-roll fashion. With a serrated knife in a sawing motion, cut into 6 equal slices. Place each into a prepared muffin cup. Bake for 15 to 20 minutes, or until lightly browned.
5. *To prepare glaze:* In a small bowl, stir together confectioners' sugar and water. Set aside.
6. Remove muffin pan to wire rack. Cool for 10 minutes before carefully removing muf-buns from cups. Cool on rack for 5 minutes. Drizzle with glaze. Serve warm. Store cooled muf-buns in an airtight container at room temperature. They are best served shortly after they are baked.

Makes 6 muf-buns

These individual mini cheesecakes are the perfect sophisticated finale to any meal.

4 ounces semisweet chocolate
About 30 chocolate sandwich cookies (enough to measure 2 cups of crumbs when crushed)
¼ cup (½ stick) unsalted butter, melted and cooled
2 teaspoons instant espresso or coffee powder
2 teaspoons water

2 packages (8 ounces each) cream cheese, at room temperature
¾ cup granulated sugar
2 large eggs, at room tempreature
1½ teaspoons vanilla extract
¼ teaspoon ground cinnamon
Sweetened whipped cream and chocolate curls, for garnish (optional)

1. Preheat oven to 350°F. Butter twelve 3 x 1¼-inch (3½- to 4-ounce) muffin cups.
2. In a microwave-safe bowl, heat chocolate in a microwave oven on High for 1 to 3 minutes, stirring halfway through cooking, until melted (or use a double boiler over hot, not simmering water). Cool at room temperature for 10 minutes.
3. Meanwhile, in container of a food processor fitted with a steel blade, process cookies until finely chopped. Scrape 2 cups of crumbs into a medium bowl. Add butter and stir to combine. Using your fingertips, firmly and evenly press mixture into bottoms and up the sides of prepared muffin cups.

4. In a small cup, stir together espresso powder and water until combined. In a large bowl, and using a hand-held electric mixer, beat cream cheese until smooth. Gradually add sugar and continue beating until light and fluffy. Beat in melted chocolate, espresso mixture, eggs, vanilla, and cinnamon until combined.

5. Divide mixture evenly among muffin cups. Bake for 15 to 20 minutes, or until set. Cool completely in pan on wire rack. Cover with plastic wrap or aluminum foil and refrigerate.

6. To serve, remove miniature cheesecakes from pan and top with whipped cream and chocolate curls, if desired.

Makes 12 muf-funs

Rich poundcake mini muffins are dipped into a fudgy chocolate fondue. Also try dipping other mini muffins, as well as marshmallows, miniature cookies, and pieces of fresh fruit and dried fruit.

POUNDCAKE MINI MUFFINS

1 cup all-purpose flour
¼ teaspoon baking powder
¼ teaspoon salt
½ cup granulated sugar
3 tablespoons unsalted butter, at room temperature

¼ cup sour cream, at room temperature
1 large egg (at room temperature), lightly beaten
1 teaspoon vanilla extract

1. Preheat oven to 350°F. Butter fifteen 1¾ x ¾-inch (about 1-ounce) miniature muffin cups.
2. In a small bowl, stir together flour, baking powder, and salt. In a large bowl, beat sugar and butter with fork until well combined. Beat in sour cream. Beat in egg and vanilla until well blended. Add dry ingredients and stir just to combine.
3. Spoon muffin batter into prepared muffin cups. Bake for 15 to 17 minutes, or until a toothpick inserted in center of one muffin comes out clean.
4. Remove muffin pan(s) to wire rack. Cool for 3 minutes before carefully removing muffins from cups; finish cooling on rack. Serve warm or cool completely and store in an airtight container at room temperature.

Makes 15 mini muffins

Chocolate Fondue

1 cup semisweet chocolate chips
½ cup heavy (whipping) cream
¼ cup light corn syrup

½ teaspoon vanilla extract or
¼ teaspoon almond extract
or more to taste

1. In a microwave-safe bowl, heat chips and cream in a microwave oven on High for 1 to 2 minutes, stirring halfway through cooking, until chocolate is melted and heated through (or use a double boiler over hot, not simmering, water). Stir in corn syrup and vanilla. If necessary, heat on High for 15 seconds, or until heated through.
2. To serve, scrape into a fondue pot to keep warm. Store leftover fondue in the refrigerator. Reheat fondue in the microwave.

Makes 1 cup

Note: One tablespoon or more coffee-flavored liqueur, orange-flavored liqueur, or cherry-flavored liqueur can be substituted for the vanilla.

An easy-to-prepare variation of the popular Italian dessert tiramisù made with, you guessed it, muffins. Use any variety of muffin that complements the coffee-flavored liqueur (chocolate works best).

8 ounces mascarpone (see note) or cream cheese, at room temperature
1 cup heavy (whipping) cream, chilled
½ cup confectioners' sugar
Generous dash salt
1 teaspoon vanilla extract
¾ cup espresso or strongly brewed coffee

2 tablespoons coffee-flavored liqueur (optional)
2 to 4 sweet muffins such as Two-Tone Chocolate Chip Muffins (page 43) or other chocolate muffins (about 8 ounces total), cut into ⅜ to ½-inch-thick slices
½ to ¾ teaspoon cocoa powder

1. In a medium bowl with a fork, beat cheese until soft. Set aside.
2. In a chilled bowl, using a hand-held electric mixer with chilled beaters, beat heavy cream, sugar, salt, and vanilla until stiff peaks form. Beat in cheese.
3. Stir together espresso and liqueur, if desired. Place half of the mixture into a small shallow bowl. Using half of the muffin slices, quickly dip each slice into espresso mixture. Do not soak. Place muffin slices, moist sides up, in bottom of an 8-inch square (2-quart) dish to make a single layer. (Do not use a metal pan.) If necessary, trim slices to fit, covering

bottom of dish. Pour slightly less than half of cheese mixture over muffin slices and spread to cover.

4. Repeat procedure with remaining muffin slices and espresso mixture. Top with remaining cheese mixture and carefully spread over top to cover.

5. Sift cocoa over top of muf-fun-misù to coat evenly. Cover and refrigerate for 4 hours, or overnight.

Makes 6 to 8 servings

Note: Mascarpone cheese, a rich Italian cheese similar to cream cheese, is found in Italian markets and many supermarkets.

If desired, sprinkle the top with 1 tablespoon or more of miniature semi-sweet chocolate chips.

This is a great way to use leftover or slightly stale muffins. Use your creativity to match muffins with mix-ins of your choice. For example, chocolate chip muffins can be combined with chopped dried tart cherries and chopped toasted almonds.

2 to 4 sweet muffins such as Two-Tone Chocolate Chip Muffins (page 43), approximately 8 ounces total, sliced vertically
½ to ¾ cup mix-ins (see note)
2 cups milk

½ cup granulated sugar
⅛ teaspoon salt
4 large eggs (at room temperature), lightly beaten
1 teaspoon vanilla extract

1. Preheat oven to 350°F. Butter a 9-inch square baking dish.
2. Place half of the muffin slices in prepared baking dish and sprinkle with mix-ins. Top with remaining muffin slices.
3. In a 2-quart saucepan, heat milk until bubbles form around edge of pan. Stir in sugar and salt. Remove from heat. Place eggs in a small bowl. Stir in ½ cup hot milk until blended. Pour egg mixture back into saucepan. Stir in vanilla. Pour over muffins and mix-ins. Press down muffins to soak with egg mixture. Place baking dish in a larger baking pan. Carefully pour enough hot water into larger pan to go 1 inch up sides of smaller pan. Bake for 50 to 60 minutes, or until a knife inserted in center comes out clean. Carefully remove baking dish. Let stand for 15 minutes. Serve warm. Store leftovers in the refrigerator up to 2 days.

Makes 6 to 8 servings

Note: Add up to ¾ cup chocolate chips, chopped nuts, and/or chopped dried fruit or raisins, depending on the type of muffins you select. Substitute up to 1 tablespoon fruit-flavored liqueur, rum, or bourbon for the vanilla extract.

To reheat pudding, place one serving in a microwave-safe container and heat in a microwave oven on Medium for 30 to 60 seconds (depending on amount of pudding), until heated through.

For Blueberry Muf-fun Puddin': Use blueberry muffins, ¾ cup fresh blueberries, and ¼ cup white chocolate chips, if desired.

Use these corn muffins in the stuffing recipe, or try other corn muffin recipes. To save time, bake the muffins one day ahead. You need about 6 cups of cubed muffins.

DOUBLE CORN MUFFINS

1¼ cups all-purpose flour
¾ cup yellow cornmeal
¼ cup sugar
2½ teaspoons baking powder
½ teaspoon salt
1 cup milk

2 large eggs (at room
**   temperature), lightly beaten**
⅓ cup vegetable oil
1 can (8¾ ounces) whole-kernel
**   corn, drained, or 1 cup**
**   fresh corn kernels**

1. Preheat oven to 400°F. Butter twelve 3 x 1¼-inch (3½- to 4-ounce) muffin cups.
2. In a large bowl, stir together flour, cornmeal, sugar, baking powder, and salt. In another bowl, stir together milk, eggs, and oil. Make a well in center of dry ingredients; add milk mixture and stir just to combine. Stir in corn.
3. Spoon batter into prepared muffin cups. Bake for 15 to 20 minutes, or until a toothpick inserted in center of one muffin comes out clean.
4. Remove muffin pan(s) to wire rack. Cool for 5 minutes before carefully removing muffins from cups; finish cooling on rack. Serve warm or cool completely and store in an airtight container at room temperature.

Makes 12 muffins

STUFFIN'

6 cups cubed corn muffins (about
  7½ muffins)
4 ounces sweet Italian sausage or
  sweet Italian turkey sausage,
  casing removed and meat
  crumbled
2 teaspoons vegetable oil
1 cup chopped onion
½ cup chopped celery
1½ cups diced apples
⅓ cup dark seedless or golden
  raisins (see note)

⅓ cup chopped pecans
¼ cup chopped parsley
¼ teaspoon dried thyme or more
  to taste
⅛ teaspoon dried sage or more to
  taste
1⅓ cups canned reduced-sodium
  chicken broth
1 large egg (at room temperature),
  lightly beaten

1. Preheat oven to 350°F. Butter a 2-quart baking dish.
2. Place muffin cubes in a jelly-roll pan. Bake for 15 minutes or until dry.
   Cool to room temperature.
3. In a nonstick medium skillet, cook sausage over medium heat, stirring
   often, about 10 minutes, or until cooked through. Drain sausage. Rinse
   and dry skillet.
4. Heat oil in skillet over medium heat. Add onion and celery; cook, stirring,
   until tender, about 8 minutes. Add apples; cook, stirring, until crisp-tender,
   about 4 minutes.
5. In a large bowl, toss together muffin cubes, sausage, onion mixture,
   raisins, nuts, parsley, thyme, and sage. Stir together broth and egg. Pour
   mixture into muffin mixture and toss to coat. Place in prepared dish.
   Cover and bake for 30 minutes. Uncover and bake for 10 minutes.

Makes about 7 cups

Note: Use all dark seedless raisins or all golden raisins instead of using two types of raisins.

Based on the popular layered cookie bars, these muffins are extra rich. Try them with your favorite combination of chips and nuts.

1½ cups graham cracker crumbs
½ cup (1 stick) unsalted butter, melted
1 can (14 ounces) sweetened condensed milk

1 cup semisweet or milk chocolate chips
1 cup white chocolate chips
1⅓ cups sweetened flaked coconut
1 cup chopped walnuts

1. Preheat oven to 350°F. Butter twelve 3 x 1¼-inch (3½- to 4-ounce) muffin cups.
2. In a medium bowl, stir together graham cracker crumbs and butter. Sprinkle the crumb mixture evenly into prepared muffin cups.
3. Pour sweetened condensed milk evenly over crumb mixture.
4. Sprinkle remaining ingredients over surface and press down. Bake 25 to 30 minutes, or until lightly browned. Remove muffin pan(s) to wire rack. Cool for 10 to 20 minutes before carefully removing muf-funs from cups; finish cooling on rack. Serve warm or cool completely and store in an airtight container at room temperature. Chill if desired.

Makes 12 muf-funs

A Tootsie Pop "ghost" haunts the top of these chocolate chip muffins.

2 cups all-purpose flour
⅔ cup firmly packed brown sugar
2 teaspoons baking powder
½ teaspoon salt
⅔ cup milk, at room temperature
½ cup (1 stick) unsalted butter,
    melted and cooled
2 large eggs (at room
    temperature), lightly beaten

2 teaspoons vanilla extract
2 cups semisweet chocolate chips
12 Tootsie Pops
Twelve 8-inch squares of white
    cloth or tissue paper
Yarn to tie ghosts onto pops

1. Preheat oven to 400°F. Butter twelve 3 x 1¼-inch (3½- to 4-ounce) muffin cups and edges surrounding the cups.
2. In a large bowl, stir together flour, sugar, baking powder, and salt. In another bowl, stir together milk, butter, eggs, and vanilla until blended. Make a well in center of dry ingredients; add milk mixture and stir just to combine. Stir in chips.
3. Spoon batter into prepared muffin cups. Bake for 15 to 20 minutes, or until a toothpick inserted in center of one muffin comes out clean.
4. Remove muffin pan(s) to wire rack. Cool for 5 minutes before carefully removing muffins from cups; finish cooling on rack.
5. Place one square of material or tissue paper on top of each pop and gather edges together around base of candy "head." Using a piece of yarn,

tie the square of cloth under the "chin." Using a marker or crayon, draw a scary face on the pop. Insert the stick of one pop into each muffin. Serve warm or cool completely and store in an airtight container at room temperature.

Makes 12 muf-funs

⚬ SPREADS ⚬

Here's a perennial favorite. It's a great use for apples you may have picked during fall apple season. (We know that we sometimes get overzealous when we go apple picking and then have a bunch of apples begging to be used.)

**8 apples, peeled, cored, and cut
into 1-inch chunks**
**1 cup apple cider or natural apple
juice**

1 teaspoon ground cinnamon
¼ teaspoon ground allspice
¼ teaspoon ground cloves
¼ teaspoon ground ginger

1. Place apples and cider in a large saucepan. Cook over medium heat, stirring occasionally, for 30 minutes, or until the apples are softened. Using a potato masher, mash the apples. Stir in the cinnamon, allspice, cloves, and ginger until combined.
2. Preheat oven to 300°F. Scrape mashed apple mixture into a 13 x 9-inch baking dish. Bake for 2 to 3 hours, stirring occasionally, until mixture has thickened. Store in an airtight container in the refrigerator.

Makes about 1 cup

This spread is delicious with Texas-Size Big Bran Muffins (page 81) and Oatmeal Raisin Muffins (page 31). Try substituting other types of preserves for the boysenberry preserves.

3 ounces cream cheese, at room temperature

3 tablespoons boysenberry or blueberry preserves

1. In a small bowl, stir together the cream cheese and boysenberry preserves until combined.
2. Serve the spread immediately or refrigerate. To serve, let stand for 15 minutes at room temperature to soften.

Makes scant ½ cup

～ BROWN SUGAR CINNAMON CREAM CHEESE ～

This simple spread goes with many of our muffins. It's also great on bagels.

½ cup whipped cream cheese
2 tablespoons firmly packed light
brown sugar

½ teaspoon ground cinnamon

In a small bowl, stir together cream cheese, sugar, and cinnamon until combined. Serve spread immediately or cover and refrigerate.
Makes approximately ½ cup

This tangy ginger spread with a hint of honey is perfect on Southern Pecan Peach Muffins (page 39) or Ginger Sweet Potato Muffins (page 95).

½ cup (1 stick) unsalted butter, at room temperature
2 tablespoons finely chopped crystallized ginger

1 tablespoon honey
Generous dash salt

1. In a small bowl, stir together butter, ginger, honey, and salt until combined.
2. Serve butter immediately or cover and refrigerate. To serve, let stand for 15 minutes at room temperature to soften.

Makes approximately ½ cup

~ COFFEE CREAM CHEESE ~

Our buddy Mary Beth Harrington, a food professional who works on recipe development for Maxwell House coffee, inspired this flavorful spread. Add more instant coffee to suit your taste.

2 teaspoons milk
¼ to ½ teaspoon instant coffee or espresso powder

½ cup whipped cream cheese
1 tablespoon granulated sugar
¼ teaspoon vanilla extract

1. In a small bowl, stir together the milk and coffee powder to dissolve. Add cream cheese, sugar, and vanilla and stir to combine.
2. Serve immediately or cover and refrigerate.
Makes approximately ½ cup

◈ ORANGE DATE NUT SPREAD ◈

A creamy spread that's great with Oatmeal Raisin Muffins (page 31) or Texas-Size Big Bran Muffins (page 81).

1 package (7½ ounces) farmer cheese
¾ cup chopped pitted dates
¼ cup chopped walnuts

1 to 2 teaspoons honey, or to taste
½ teaspoon grated orange peel
¼ teaspoon vanilla extract

1. Place cheese, dates, nuts, honey, orange peel, and vanilla in container of food processor fitted with a steel blade; process 30 to 60 seconds, or until desired consistency, stopping to scrape down sides of container with rubber scraper, if necessary.
2. Remove spread to a small bowl. Serve immediately or cover and refrigerate. To serve, let stand for 15 minutes at room temperature to soften.

Makes scant 1⅓ cups

✎ PARMESAN BUTTER ✎

Here's a delicious butter that's great served with many of the muffins and also on baked potatoes! Try it with Parmesan Prosciutto Mini Muffins (page 61).

½ cup (1 stick) unsalted butter, at
    room temperature
⅓ cup freshly grated Parmesan
    cheese

Dash hot pepper sauce

1. In a small bowl, stir together butter, cheese, and pepper sauce until combined.
2. Serve immediately or cover and refrigerate. To serve, let stand for 15 minutes at room temperature to soften.

Makes a generous ½ cup

❧ ROASTED GARLIC SPREAD ❧

Serve this savory spread with Spud Muffins (page 41) or Double Corn Muffins (page 127). It's also great on bagels and baked potatoes.

1 very large head garlic
1 teaspoon olive oil
4 ounces cream cheese, at room temperature

2 tablespoons unsalted butter, at room temperature
Dash salt
Dash ground black pepper

1. Preheat oven to 350°F.
2. Place whole garlic head in a small baking dish and drizzle with oil. Cover with aluminum foil. Bake for 45 minutes or until tender. Cool for 10 minutes in dish. Remove and cool completely. Squeeze garlic cloves out of skins. Mash or finely chop roasted garlic to measure 2 tablespoons, or more to taste. (Leftover roasted garlic can be spread on bread or mixed into mashed potatoes.)
3. In a small bowl, cream together garlic, cream cheese, butter, salt, and pepper until blended. Serve immediately, or store in an airtight container in the refrigerator. To serve, let stand for 15 minutes at room temperature to soften.

Makes approximately ⅔ cup

Goat Cheese Variation: Substitute 2 ounces chèvre (fresh soft goat cheese) for half of the cream cheese and omit salt.

❧ Index ❧

145